Beyond the Binary

Beyond the Binary

Thinking about Sex and Gender

Shannon Dea

broadview press

BROADVIEW PRESS— www.broadviewpress.com
Peterborough, Ontario, Canada

Founded in 1985, Broadview Press remains a wholly independent publishing house.
Broadview's focus is on academic publishing; our titles are accessible to university and col-
lege students as well as scholars and general readers. With over 600 titles in print, Broadview
has become a leading international publisher in the humanities, with world-wide distribution.
Broadview is committed to environmentally responsible publishing and fair business practices.

The interior of this book is printed on 100% recycled paper.

Library and Archives Canada Cataloguing in Publication

Dea, Shannon, 1969–, author
    Beyond the binary : thinking about sex and gender / Shannon Dea.

Includes bibliographical references and index.
ISBN 978-1-55481-283-7 (paperback)

    1. Sex. 2. Sex (Biology). 3. Sex differences. 4. Gender identity.
I. Title.

HQ1075.D42 2016   305.3   C2016-901676-5

Broadview Press handles its own distribution in North America
PO Box 1243, Peterborough, Ontario K9J 7H5, Canada
555 Riverwalk Parkway, Tonawanda, NY 14150, USA
Tel: (705) 743-8990; Fax: (705) 743-8353
email: customerservice@broadviewpress.com

Distribution is handled by Eurospan Group in the UK, Europe, Central Asia, Middle East,
Africa, India, Southeast Asia, Central America, South America, and the Caribbean. Distribution
is handled by Footprint Books in Australia and New Zealand.

Broadview Press acknowledges the financial support of the Government of Canada through
the Canada Book Fund for our publishing activities.

Edited by Robert M. Martin
Book design by Michel Vrana

PRINTED IN CANADA

For my mother, Shirley Dea,
who gave me books, pencils and paper, and the desire to
do something good with them.

Contents

Illustrations

Preface

This volume is designed to provide students with a multi-disciplinary background to current debates about sex and gender in the life sciences, medicine, and public policy.

In recent years, neuroscientists, geneticists, and evolutionists, among others, have engaged in lively debate over the fixity of biological sex categories. In neuroscience, for instance, scholars such as Simon Baron-Cohen argue that male and female brains are physically different from each other (and hence that men and women are inherently different from one another), while on the other side neurofeminists such as Cordelia Fine point to implicit biases that they allege vitiate the methodology and results of the "brain sex" scientists. Parallel debates are occurring within genetics, evolutionary science and other life sciences. Within the public sphere, a readership ill-trained to parse the above debates and science journalists under increasing pressure to boil science news down to clickbait too often extrapolate from parries in the sex science debates to hasty conclusions about gender.

In response, researchers from across the humanities and social sciences have, over the past thirty years, developed a rich critical sex studies movement. However, the results of this work have been slow to trickle down to instructional materials. While scholarly monographs and journal articles that problematize folk assumptions about the metaphysics and epistemology of sex and gender are regularly published, the bulk of undergraduate textbooks in the area continue to focus instead on normative—that is, on ethical and socio-political—issues.

In 2007, when I first began teaching an undergraduate (Philosophy and Women's Studies) course on sex and gender, I wanted to focus on classificatory questions, like the following: *What is sex? What is gender? What is the relationship between those two categories? How many sexes are there? How many genders? Are sex and gender categories biological inevitabilities or historically contingent?* Since no undergraduate textbook focused exclusively on these questions, I created my own course reader that anthologized texts from a wide range of disciplines, from ancient times to the present. Next, I wrote a series of course notes to accompany the texts. For the present volume, I have adapted those course notes so that they no longer assume that students are reading the primary texts I started with. The result, I hope, is a broad, accessible undergraduate level introduction to the metaphysics of sex and gender.

The volume is distinctive in its attention to sex as a category. Many philosophy of sex/gender textbooks emphasize gender, ethical issues relating to gender, sexual orientation, and sexual activity. While all of these usual emphases are, to be sure, very important (and while the book touches on all of these matters in one way or another), it is also crucial to consider what we know—or think we know—about the biological divisions underlying them. Of course, our understanding of these biological divisions bears upon how we think about those other matters. Questions about sexual orientation, for instance, arguably become more complicated in the case of intersex or trans people. This textbook is designed to allow you to identify and engage these fundamental questions in a rigorous, philosophically robust way.

This book is also noteworthy for the breadth of periods, disciplines, and views upon which it draws. It surveys ideas and arguments from the canons of philosophy, religion, the social and life sciences, literature, and literary theory. The source texts upon which the volume draws range from 900 BCE to the present. One of the abiding lessons that I hope you will take away from reading this book is that metaphysical questions about sex and gender have been raised for centuries and across many traditions by some of the greatest thinkers of all time. Aristotle was just as interested in biological sex as were radical thinkers from the last century—even if his conclusions about it were very different from theirs.

The volume is divided into 12 chapters:

1. Introduction
2. Methodology and Terminology
3. Aristotelian and Judeo-Christian Models of Sex Difference
4. The Second Sex
5. The Third Sex
6. The Third Gender
7. Intersex
8. Trans Issues
9. Biodeterminism
10. The One-Sex Model
11. Difference and Equality
12. Sex/Gender as Social Construction

As you work through these chapters, you will employ a range of scholarly methods and evaluate arguments for a variety of different conclusions. There is no sense in which any chapter—or the volume as a whole—purports to give you the "right answers." In each chapter, you will be exposed to a range of views and data about which you will be invited to think critically. To facilitate such critical thinking, each chapter features a number of provocative questions for reflection and discussion. In case you wish to pursue more in-depth study of the material in any of the chapters, each chapter concludes with recommendations for further reading. A glossary of terms, an annotated bibliography, and an index round out the volume.

Whether you read this textbook on its own, or it tandem with some of the readings recommended at the end of each chapter, I hope that you will come away from it with a deepened understanding of the complexity of sex and gender categories, but also of the diverse ways in which cognate questions are engaged within and across different disciplines and historical periods.

Acknowledgements

I developed the textbook for an online course, based on my lectures from the on-campus version of the same course. I am very grateful to the hundreds of students I taught over the years in the original on-campus course, each of whom in some way helped to shape the development of the book. I am likewise grateful to the students and graders for the online course for their useful comments. Thanks in particular to Jim Jordan and Kirsten MacDonald for many helpful conversations we had about the book. Warm thanks, too, to Stephen Latta at Broadview for his patient encouragement to publish the volume, and to three anonymous Broadview referees for their thoughtful suggestions. I am grateful to Bob Martin for his careful, erudite, and witty editing, and to Broadview's Merilee Atos for her invaluable assistance obtaining image permissions. Thank you to Eric Olofson and Jennifer Saul for helpful advice on content, and to Tim Kenyon and Dave DeVidi for confidence in me that sometimes exceeded my own. I am grateful to Molly Dea-Stephenson for her acute and generous reading of the penultimate version of the manuscript and to Mark Stephenson for his inexhaustible support and encouragement over the years. Finally, I owe a huge debt of gratitude to the staff at

University of Waterloo's Centre for Extended Learning, and to my colleague, Gerry Callaghan. Gerry spent hours poring over the early manuscript before it even looked like a manuscript and offered sage advice that substantially improved the final version. It is no exaggeration to say that without Gerry's contribution, there would be no book.

Those to whom I extend my thanks share in the credit for any merits of the volume; the responsibility for its faults rests on me alone.

CHAPTER 1

Introduction

1.1. What's so complicated about sex and gender categories?

In this textbook, we consider some of the deepest theoretical and practical questions about sex and gender. Its central emphasis is the relationship between gender, understood as a psycho-socio-cultural category, and biological sex, understood as a type of physiological classification. It will perhaps come as no surprise that much of our past and current discourse on gender attests to close relationships between gender and biological sex categories—consider, for example, the common association of the gender descriptors "masculine" and "feminine" with the biological categories of "male" and "female." What is perhaps more surprising is just how complicated the relationships between the biological domain of sex and the socio-cultural domain of gender turn out to be. As we'll see, the distinctions between sex and gender, and between biology and culture/society/psychology, are neither tidy nor intuitive. One of the lessons of this volume is that, for human beings, there is no biology without society (and vice versa!). The notion that gender is fluid and malleable is nowadays quite familiar. It turns out that sex too is a complicated business—and always has been.

At first glance, there may seem to be little difficulty in categorizing most people into two groups—male and female—according to their physical features. After all, it happens all the time on public restroom doors. However, the iconography of male and female stick-people on public toilets does not do justice to the rich array of biological features that must be taken into account when we classify people according to their sex—genetics, hormones, gonadal tissue, primary anatomical sex traits (like penises and vaginas), secondary anatomical sex traits (like square jaws and wide hips), reproductive functions, and more. While most people are in most of these respects exclusively male or exclusively female, it is not true of everybody. Moreover, even though, in our social lives, we tend to judge people's sex by their secondary sex traits, there is wide variation in these traits' instantiation within human populations. More seriously perhaps, even if all human beings were uncontroversially male or female in every one of the biological respects I have mentioned, it is still not at all clear what kind of category sex is. Is it a natural kind like lead or gold? Or a convenient heuristic for sorting organisms based on a collection of loosely related, but distinct, properties?

You might be wondering what exactly is so complicated about sex categories. Isn't the male/female distinction pretty straightforward? Throughout this book, you'll encounter plenty of material that problematizes the "sex" part of "sex categories," but before we get to that, it's worth noticing how complicated the "category" part is.

1.2. Essences and natural kinds

In Chapter 3, we will take a look at Aristotle's metaphysics. Aristotle's influential view is that everything that exists has a single defining feature that makes it the kind of thing that it is. He calls this defining feature an *essence*. For Aristotle, the essence of a plant is to nourish itself, the essence of an animal is to perceive, and the essence of a human being is to reason. While this view is in many ways an attractive one, it is just not clear that things really have such singular defining features. The better we get to know the world, the more we discover exceptions to the features that we take to define things. For instance, while live births seem to be defining of mammals, and flight seems to be defining of birds, some mammals (such as the platypus and the spiny anteater) lay eggs and some birds (like penguins and ostriches) cannot fly.

Indeed, while biologists inevitably use such features as egg-laying and flight as heuristics to help identify species, the most common way of understanding species today does not rest on such features. For many contemporary biologists, species are definable not in terms of essential traits but in terms of reproduction. Whether they highly resemble each other or not, two individuals belong to the same species if they can mate and produce fertile offspring. Despite the considerable differences between them, Chihuahuas and Great Danes belong to the same species because they can produce fertile offspring. By contrast, horses and donkeys, despite their similarity, cannot produce fertile offspring. Mules—the offspring of horse-donkey pairings—cannot themselves reproduce.

While few philosophers today agree with Aristotle's view about essences, many philosophers find it useful to conceptualize categories in terms of *natural kinds*. As the name suggests, counting a category as a natural kind rests on two main criteria: the category must be *natural*, and it must be a *kind*. The naturalness criterion is simply that the kind must be a kind in virtue of features of reality independent of human perception. I might see a face in the bark of a tree, but any connection between the face in the tree and real faces is reducible to my own perception. There is in this sense no natural connection between tree-faces and real faces. The kind criterion requires that two naturally connected things only share in a natural kind if they really are the same *kind* of thing. A brown tree and a brown horse really do share the property of being brown quite apart from anyone's perception of them. Their shared brownness is in this sense natural. However, brownness isn't enough to make a horse and a tree the same kind of thing. When philosophers ask what categories are natural kinds, they are asking what categories pick out real kinds of things bound together by natural, mind-independent properties. Chemical elements such as gold and chemical compounds such as H^2O are often regarded as paradigmatic examples of natural kinds. However, even those philosophers who agree that there exist natural kinds disagree about whether biological categories such as species or sex constitute natural kinds.

A 1968 novel by American author Cormac McCarthy offers an amusing example of the kind of categorial questions we have been exploring. In one memorable scene in *Outer Dark*, the central character, Holme, encounters a hog herder with a large herd of hogs. The herder tells Holme that many of the hogs in the herd belong to the mulefoot breed, so-named because mulefoot hogs have uncloven hooves like mules rather than the cloven hooves that are typical of swine. The herder explains to Holme that pork isn't kosher precisely because of pigs' cloven hooves, and wonders aloud whether the Biblical injunction against eating pigs applies to mulefoot hogs:

> Well is he a hog or ain't he? Accordin to the bible.
> I'd say a hog was a hog if he didn't have nary feet a-tall.
> I might do it myself, the drover said, because if he was to have feet you'd look for em to be hog's feet. Like if ye had a hog didn't have no head you'd know it for a hog anyways. But if ye seen one walkin around with a mule's head on him ye might be puzzled.[1]

In this exchange, Holme and the hog-herder debate a question as old as Aristotle: what specific features entitle an individual to membership in a particular category? Must an animal have cloven hooves to count as a hog? Or, is it enough that it not have mulefeet? Or, is the category "hog" sufficiently flexible to include animals with a range of different types of feet? Surely, flexible categories are best able to cope with the broad range of variations that occur within biological populations.

1.3. Ambiguities, redundancies, and deficiencies

On the other hand, too much flexibility means that our categories don't do any useful work for us. In Argentinian writer Jorge Luis Borges's "The Analytical Language of John Wilkins," Borges refers

---

1   Cormac McCarthy, *Outer Dark*, 215.

to "a certain Chinese encyclopedia entitled *Celestial Emporium of Benevolent Knowledge*"; he illustrates the fictitious encyclopedia's "ambiguities, redundancies, and deficiencies" by quoting its division of animals into:

(a) those that belong to the Emperor, (b) embalmed ones, (c) those that are trained, (d) suckling pigs, (e) mermaids, (f) fabulous ones, (g) stray dogs, (h) those that are included in this classification, (i) those that tremble as if they were mad, (j) innumerable ones, (k) those drawn with a very fine camel's hair brush, (l) others, (m) those that have just broken a flower vase, (n) those that resemble flies from a distance.[2]

This oft-quoted excerpt from Borges derives its fame from the fact that French philosopher Michel Foucault opens his book *The Order of Things* by quoting and discussing the passage. "In the wonderment of this taxonomy," Foucault writes, "the thing we apprehend in one great leap, the thing that, by means of the fable, is demonstrated as the exotic charm of another system of thought, is the limitation of our own, the stark impossibility of thinking *that*."[3]

Most of Borges's fanciful categories *work*, in the sense that we'd know more or less how to populate them, if we encountered the appropriate animals. (The exceptions might be "those that are included in this classification" and "other," which are a bit trickier to wrangle.) However, the oddness of the classifications forces us to examine exactly what they are meant to accomplish. What utility could there be in classifying animals that tremble as if they were mad? Or those who have just broken a flower vase? One can of course imagine uses. A prospective horseback rider might well wish to distinguish between the horses that tremble as if mad and the calm ones, and a pet owner might want to locate animals that have just knocked over a flower vase in order to dry their paws before they track wet through the house. However, these uses are specific to very particular contexts. One of the surprising things about the

---

2   Jorge Luis Borges, "The Analytical Language of John Wilkins," 103.
3   Michel Foucault, *The Order of Things*, xv.

classification Borges invents is the way that it elevates such *ad hoc*, local requirements into an overarching classificatory scheme.

> Many, if not all, classificatory schemes serve practical purposes. It can be instructive to remind ourselves of some of the serious consequences of these purposes. Consider, for instance, the effect that sex categories have on livestock. Chicken sexers are people trained to sort baby chicks based on sex. For egg-laying breeds, only the females are required. So, most of the male chicks are killed and turned into pet food or fertilizer. The situation is similar for dairy cattle. Again, since only the female calves will grow up to produce milk, most of the males are slaughtered for veal meat. Take a few moments to reflect on whether there are similarly serious advantages or disadvantages for humans of being sexed male or female.

Another reason that we feel in the encounter with Borges's classification "the stark impossibility of thinking *that*" is that most of the categories in the list are orthogonal to each other—that is, they pick out different kinds of things about animals, rather than contrasting mutually exclusive traits. The very same animal may at once be belonging to the Emperor, embalmed, and a suckling pig. Thus, this classification no more sorts animals into distinct groups than the categories *female, brown-haired,* and *artistic* sort people. (After all, the very same person may be female, brown-haired, and artistic.)

You might think that no one outside of fiction would ever adopt a classificatory system that both entrenches ad hoc, context-specific usages and combines orthogonal categories. However, as we will see in the remainder of this volume, some scholars and activists argue that the standard sex categories of male and female (not to mention the gender categories of man and woman, boy and girl, masculine and feminine) do just that. While it is arguably important to distinguish male from female human beings if one wishes to reproduce sexually, it is not at all clear that this distinction should have any bearing upon, say, which public bathroom one uses. To extend a classification useful for biological reproduction to such cultural matters as restroom habits may seem to elevate an ad hoc category in much the same way that Borges's list does.

As for the orthogonal categories, male and female themselves include a range of sub-categories, including (but not limited to) morphology, physiological function, chromosomal character, and hormonal production/reception. For most of us, these categories largely overlap, such that (for instance) one has a male morphology, male physiological functions, and XY chromosomes, and moreover produces large quantities of androgens to which tissue responds in typically male ways. Because of this common overlap, it is easy to forget that these sub-categories don't align for everybody.

You may have heard about the case of Caster Semenya, a top South African runner who, it turns out, has XY (i.e., male) sex chromosomes, but female morphology because her tissues are not responsive to androgens. Our traditional sex categories are, arguably, unequal to the challenge of classifying people like Semenya, in large part because, as people like Semenya make clear, our sex categories are themselves made up of several orthogonal classifications.

As you work through the book and encounter a number of different possible classificatory schemes for sex and gender, remember to ask yourself: What work is this category doing? Does it elevate a specific usage into an overarching classificatory scheme? Is this category simple or complex? If it is complex, are its subcategories orthogonal with each other?

1.4 Sex and gender as genres

Let us conclude our consideration of approaches to categorization by considering an example from contemporary media.

Today, lots of people get their entertainment media from online movie and music streaming services, such as Netflix and Pandora. In general, such services use two distinct methods to recommend shows or songs to users—categorizing content by genre, and generating predictions about what content users will enjoy based on what content they consumed and enjoyed in the past. The first method is stipulative, the second is statistical. Let's talk about each of these approaches to categorization in turn.

The stipulative approach depends on someone stipulating in advance what genres exist, what relation obtains between those genres, and what content belongs in each genre. Is pop/rock a halfway point between pop and rock, or a subcategory of pop, rock, or both? Is Kendrick Lamar hip hop or avant-garde jazz? Can a single artist be both East Coast hip hop and West Coast hip hop, or must they be one or the other? The end-user of streaming services doesn't need to worry too much about these questions since online services by their nature possess useful search functions, and allow considerable cross-referencing. However, this user-friendliness is the result of the platform, not the categories themselves. If you have ever gone looking for a particular artist or title in a bricks and mortar CD/DVD store, you will have on occasion found yourself asking exactly the type of categorial questions listed above. Should you look for *The Cabinet of Doctor Caligari* in the classic film section, the horror section, or the imports section? It seems that for every artist or film that fits neatly into a category, there is another that resists tidy categorization.

Many users of streaming services have as much or more luck finding movies and songs they like by way of the custom suggestions offered to them by the streaming services. These recommendations are generated not by stipulation but statistically. If I liked films X, Y, and Z, then there is a good chance that I'll enjoy a fourth film that was popular with other admirers of X, Y, and Z.

Categorizing sex and gender traits might be a bit like categorizing music or movies. One option is to stipulate that there exist certain sex and gender categories, and then handle case by case sex or gender expressions that straddle or fall outside of the categories. Another option is to take a statistical approach, noticing common clusters of sex and gender traits and using these patterns as heuristics without attributing to them any deeper reality. Which approach do you think better aligns with the range of sex and gender expressions extant? What advantages and disadvantages does each approach offer?

1.5. Questions for reflection

- What difference do you think a hog's feet make to whether it counts as a hog or not? If not feet, do hogs have any other features or parts that you consider "essential" to them counting as hogs? Are there analogous features or parts that dictate which animals count as male or female? Does an animal have to have a penis to count as male, for instance? (Note that in 97 per cent of bird species, males do not have penises.)

- If a human being is male in one respect (chromosomally, say) and female in another (perhaps morphologically), ought we to count them as male or female? Why? Which sex sub-categories should be the arbiters in cases like this?
- Think about the uses to which sex and gender categories for human beings are put. Are they inevitable, or do they vary from culture to culture? Illustrate your answer with examples.

1.6. Works cited and recommended reading

Borges, Jorge Luis. "The Analytical Language of John Wilkins." *Other Inquisitions: 1937–1952*. Trans. Ruth Simms. London: Souvenir Press, 1973. 101–05.

Foucault, Michel. *The Order of Things: An Archaeology of the Human Sciences*. New York: Vintage, 1994.

McCarthy, Cormac. *Outer Dark*. New York: Vintage, 1993.

CHAPTER 2

Methodology
and Terminology

2.1 Discourse and geneaology

In this chapter, we consider methodological approaches and terminology that will assist us in our exploration of sex and gender.

It is arguably impossible to undertake the study of sex and
gender without some awareness of the work of the great French
philosopher and social scientist, Michel Foucault (1926–84). His
ambitious three volume *History of Sexuality* (1976) is primarily
concerned with the activity of sex rather than sexual taxonomies
(that is, it is about *having sex*, not *belonging to a sex*). However,
the stance that it adopts in its treatment of sexuality is one that
informs much that we will do in this volume.

As a scholar, Foucault analyzes *discursive practices* in order to
try to discern the nature of the system of power that is reproduced
within those practices. What Foucault means by a discursive practice is complicated; we shall use a simplified version of his notion,
taking it to be a habitual means of conveying meaning. It might
be linguistic, but it needn't be. Newspaper columns, for instance,
constitute one set of discursive practices. This just means that there
are conventions that newspaper columnists tend to follow when they

11

produce their columns. The practice of shaking hands when you meet someone is another kind of discursive practice. Even though, unlike a newspaper column, shaking hands does not involve language, it nonetheless communicates meaning from one person to the next, and indeed is intended to do so.

Foucault's hypothesis is that all social practices, including discursive practices, reflect the nature of the society in which they are produced, and in particular they reflect the nature of power relations within that society. Moreover, they often do so unconsciously and unintentionally.

In his analysis of discursive practices, Foucault seeks to discover what ideology—and, hence, what sort of system of power—explains our particular discursive practices. That is, he regards those practices *as practices* and as constituting indirect evidence about the nature of the societal power that influences us. The evidence is indirect because, on Foucault's view, the underlying power relations are seldom obvious or "out in the open," and thus they resist inspection by more direct means of examination.

Foucault's notion of underlying power relations of which we are not consciously aware has its roots in the neo-Marxist conception of *ideology*. While the word "ideology" often gets used in common parlance to mean something neutral like "a set of ideas someone possesses," the neo-Marxist use of the term is much more specific. "Ideology," in the neo-Marxist sense, refers to a set of ideas, particular to a political system, that informs the thoughts, actions and utterances of people living within that system without their being aware of it. So, for instance, poor people in the West might work overtime because they are under the sway of a liberal capitalist ideology that holds (among other things) that hard work is always rewarded, and that anyone can succeed if they work hard enough. What makes this ideology, as opposed to just an idea, is that the view I've just described permeates liberal capitalist societies. Members of those societies hold the view not because they arrived at it on their own, but because they unconsciously buy into their society's dominant way of thinking. To put it crudely, neo-Marxists regard us as more or less unfree with respect to ideology.

> We do not freely choose those ideas; they are impressed upon us by the system of power we occupy. Just as seriously, we may not even be aware of the fact that we hold such views, or that we are influenced by them. On the Marxist account, ideology is the water in which we swim. We do not notice it because it is ubiquitous, but it affects everything we do and think.

Foucault's project is not epistemological but (in his own terminology) *genealogical*. That is, when he examines what is said—a bit of discourse—he is not mainly concerned with the epistemological question of whether or not it is true, and how we might know this. Rather, he wants to know how particular forms of discursive practice arise, and what leads us (apart from truth) to engage in these forms of discourse. For Foucault, that an utterance is true does not on its own explain why we make the utterance. After all, there is an infinite collection of true statements we could make about the world that we never do make. For instance, while it is true that I have ten toes, in general, I don't announce it. Even when we are speaking the truth, we tend to do so for some practical reason. Thus, if a detective were searching for a nine-toed murder suspect, I would have a practical reason to announce that I have ten toes. If we only focus on the truth of the claim and ignore the motivation for it, we miss an important part of the story.

What is the point of Foucault's "genealogical" project? In short, he seeks to uncover in discourse the workings of power.

In *History of Sexuality*, Foucault is especially concerned with our discursive practices when it comes to sex. He opens the book by describing the so-called repressive hypothesis, the idea that human beings (or, at least, Europeans) were more sexually open until the beginning of the seventeenth century, at which time sexuality came to be repressed in a variety of ways as part of early modern imperialist society.

According to the repressive hypothesis, this repression reached its peak in Victorian society. As we might expect, Foucault is less interested in whether or not the repressive hypothesis is true than in what people's motivations are for propounding the hypothesis. What practical reasons might there be for post-Victorians to describe the history of sexuality in this way? For Foucault, then, the real question is not "Why are we repressed?" but "Why do we say that we are repressed?"

Foucault raises "three serious doubts" about the repressive hypothesis, each of which is posed in the form of a pointed question:

> 1. "Is sexual repression truly an established historical fact?" (He calls this the historical question.)
> 2. "Do the workings of power, and in particular those mechanisms that are brought into play in societies such as ours, really belong primarily to the category of repression?" (The historico-theoretical question.)
> 3. "Did the critical discourse that addresses itself to repression come to act as a roadblock to a power mechanism that had operated unchallenged up to that point, or is it not in fact part of the same historical network as the thing it denounces (and doubtless misrepresents) by calling it 'repression'?" (The historico-political question.)[1]

Many readers find Foucault's writing difficult and elusive, and with good reason. He often adopts an ironic tone, and his rhetorical purpose is frequently provocative rather than straightforwardly communicative. Frustratingly, the clearest and most accessible of Foucault's three serious doubts—the first one—is the one he cares least about. For Foucault, the question of whether the repressive hypothesis is true is ultimately a distraction from the two more complicated issues he raises in the second and third doubts.

Foucault's second doubt hints that power may in fact be exercised just as much through permission—encouragement to act in a certain way—as through repression—inhibition from acting in a certain way. To make sense of this idea, imagine the ways that a landscape architect might seek to confine people to a particular area in a park. Of course, she might erect fences and barricades and "do not enter" signs. However, it might be just as effective for her to lure people to the desired area by means of benches, bridges and attractive ponds. Notice that both sets of mechanisms—both

---

1   Michel Foucault, *The History of Sexuality*, 10.

permission and repression—are means of bringing about the same result—they are both means of exercising power. Crucially though, we enjoy receiving permission, and resent being prohibited from doing things. People typically yell "You're not my boss!" when they are prevented from doing things, not when they are encouraged. Thus, positive mechanisms may be more effective than repression in the exercise of power since we are less likely to rebel against, or indeed *notice*, permission as opposed to repression.

In his final doubt, Foucault raises the further worry that critiques of supposed injustices can end up reproducing the assumptions that underlie those injustices. Here is a contemporary example to illustrate the subtle point Foucault is driving at. In recent decades, we have seen a dramatic increase in popular and legislative support for same-sex marriage. The original motivation for this movement concerned familial rights. Same-sex couples who were denied the legal status accorded to married couples were consequently denied familial pension and benefit coverage, were often prohibited from adopting children, and were sometimes even prevented from visiting their partners in hospital. Activists criticized this unequal treatment of same-sex and opposite-sex couples, and have since been remarkably successful in securing marital rights for same-sex couples. However, in the spirit of Foucault's third serious doubt, one might raise the concern that extending the benefits associated with marriage to same-sex couples has inadvertently served to reinforce marriage—originally a heterosexual institution and one that arguably remains in many respects heteronormative—as the sole legitimate form of "immediate family." From that point of view, critiquing the exclusivity of marriage resulted in the assimilation of other forms of family life rather than in a genuine broadening of possibilities to include such alternative forms of family as those in which an unmarried child lives with and provides care for an aging parent, or two siblings or close friends cohabit and support each other for decades. Foucault might therefore caution that critics of marriage inequality ended up unintentionally supporting the very system of power they aimed to critique.

If we combine Foucault's second and third "serious doubts," we can arrive at the following Foucauldian advice: If you want to study the expression of power in your society, you must attend not only to prohibition, but also—and perhaps especially—to permission and critique. If we wish to understand power—and in particular the ubiquitous power that we do not even notice precisely because we are constituted by it—then we must examine instances of all three of these types of discursive practices and ask ourselves what sort of system of power would produce them.

How does this method of analysis, which Foucault applies generally throughout his *corpus*, but which in *The History of Sexuality* he particularly applies to the kind of sex that we have, bear upon the kind of sex we are here interested in—sex as a category?

Recall the ten toes example from earlier in this discussion. Now imagine a society in which there are two kinds of public restrooms—those for people with exactly ten toes, and those for people with more or fewer than ten toes. What kind of society would orient itself such that separate spaces are allocated to people depending on how many toes they have? Presumably, a society in which, for whatever reason, toe orthodoxy was a central, organizing value. Recalling the insights from the second and third serious doubts, we might expect to see that value playing out in the society's prohibitions ("No nine toesers allowed!"), its prescriptions ("Sale! Toe-ectomies! Finally, you too can be ten-toed!"), and its critiques ("These toeist hiring practices are unjust and illegal!").

Of course, we do not live in a society that centrally organizes itself around the value of toe orthodoxy. However, as countless real prohibitions, prescriptions, and critiques from the real world make clear, our society does to a very great extent organize itself around various norms concerning sex and gender.

As you work through this volume, you will have many opportunities to examine the ways in which our society is organized around sex and gender norms. First though, we have a bit more groundwork to do.

2.2. Intersectionality: Power exerting itself in many directions at once

We have just seen that, for Foucault, discursive analysis helps us to uncover the system of power in which we are enmeshed. When we start to take that system seriously, it becomes clear that each of us is differently located within it. People are advantaged or disadvantaged because of their gender, race, ethnicity, class, sexual orientation, religion, disability, citizenship, etc. For instance, I experience some disadvantage because I am a woman who grew up in the working class. However, I enjoy privileges associated with being straight and white. While a Black lesbian and I are both subject to some discrimination because of our gender, she is subject to further discrimination due to her race and sexual orientation. Put simply, there is no common "women's experience."

Despite this, activism often takes a single-axis approach, with distinct solidarity groups for women, Black people, LGBTQ[2] people, etc. Of course, no one is only a woman, or only Black, or only gay. We belong to many groups. For this reason, a single-axis approach to discrimination tends to further marginalize the most disadvantaged members of solidarity groups. Feminists, for instance, are often justly criticized for wrongly assuming that the experience of white, middle-class Western women is typical of all women. When feminists primarily advocate for white middle-class Western women, the conditions for women of colour and women in the so-called Global South are overlooked. Similarly, African American political action has often centred on men, thereby further disadvantaging Black women.

In 1989, Black feminist lawyer and legal scholar Kimberlé Crenshaw developed the concept of *intersectionality* to address this phenomenon. She had observed a troubling trend in the law. When Black women sued their employers for discriminatory practices, those employers were able to defend themselves successfully by adducing evidence that they did not in fact discriminate against women or Black people. However, the women whom they were treating well were white, and the Black people they were treating well were men. Black women were the subject of discrimination, but it was impossible to argue this on a single-axis approach. As Crenshaw explains,

---

2   LGBTQ is one of the various acronyms used to refer to the so-called queer community. It stands for "Lesbian, Gay, Bisexual, Transgender" and "Queer" (or sometimes "Questioning"). In Chapters 6, 7, and 8, we'll briefly look at longer acronyms related to this one.

[D]ominant conceptions of discrimination condition us to think about subordination as disadvantage occurring along a single categorical axis.... [T]his single-axis framework erases Black women in the conceptualization, identification and remediation of race and sex discrimination by limiting enquiry to the experiences of otherwise-privileged members of the group. In other words, in race discrimination cases, discrimination tends to be viewed in terms of sex- or class-privileged Blacks; in sex discrimination cases, the focus is on race- and class-privileged women.[3]

An intersectional approach, by contrast, offers a framework with which to analyze each person's location in the intersecting array of inequities. Adopting such a framework, argues Crenshaw, allows us to address the most acute injustices, and the most acutely disadvantaged people. "[P]lacing those who currently are marginalized in the center," she tells us, "is the most effective way to resist efforts to compartmentalize experiences and undermine potential collective action."[4]

As you work through this book, remember to consider the intersection of gender with other axes of identity. Ask yourself: Whose account of gender is this? Who is included in the account? Who is effaced by it?

2.3. Gender as gender attribution

People often use the terms "sex" and "gender" interchangeably. However, many scholars and activists use "sex" to refer to a biological category involving chromosomes, hormones, anatomical features, etc., reserving "gender" for socio-cultural-psychological matters such as dress, behaviour, and identity. In their ground-breaking 1978 work, *Gender: An Ethnomethodological Approach*, psychologists Kessler and McKenna propose instead that we reserve "sex" for the activity and use "gender" for the taxonomy (whether biological

---

3   Kimberlé Crenshaw, "Demarginalizing the Intersection of Race and Sex: A Black Feminist Critique of Antidiscrimination Doctrine, Feminist Theory and Antiracist Politics," 140.
4   Crenshaw, 167.

or socio-cultural-psychological). Perhaps unsurprisingly, "gender" turns out, for them, to be an extremely rich term.

In order to disambiguate the separate concepts that, on their view, get conflated in the broad category of gender, they offer a lexicon of gender terms, all grounded in the concept of *gender attribution*. While we may not wish to adopt Kessler and McKenna's practice of using "gender" even for biological matters, some of the subsidiary terms they define will be useful for us in the remainder of this volume. Before we get to them, though, a word or two about gender attribution.

"Gender attribution" is the term that Kessler and McKenna use for the decision we make about a person's gender when we first see that person. Kessler and McKenna argue that we are constantly attributing genders to people. We do so without really trying, and are often unaware that we are even doing it.

As we walk down the street or look around a classroom, we often cannot help mentally ticking off "he," "she," "she," "she," "he," "he" as we see people. Usually, we don't become aware of this process of gender attribution until we encounter difficulty in making the attribution due to a mixture of (traditionally) masculine and feminine cues, or an absence of them. In our gender attributions, most of us assume that people are either male or female, but not neither or both. However, as Kessler and McKenna point out, even in easy, uncontroversial gender attributions, none of the cues we use are always and without exception true of only one gender. Some women have beards, for instance, and some men have breasts. Lots of women wear short hair and trousers; some men wear long hair and skirts.

While gender attribution often feels like a mere inspection process, Kessler and McKenna hold that, given the complexity of the cues involved and the difficulty of interpreting them, it is more than an inspection. Indeed, it is a decision. That is, we do not simply notice someone's gender; we determine it. In the process of deciding people's genders, they argue, we construct a world of "two, and only two, genders."[5]

---

5   Suzanne Kessler and Wendy McKenna, *Gender: An Ethnomethodological Approach*, 3.

Kessler and McKenna's Guiding Question

"How, in any interaction, is a sense of the reality of a world of two, and only two, genders constructed? How do we "do" gender attributions? That is, what kinds of rules do we apply to what kinds of displays, such that in every concrete instance we produce a sense that there are only men and women, and that this is an objective fact...."[6]

Kessler and McKenna reveal the scope and complexity of gender attribution as a concept by proposing a set of terms defined via gender attribution. Many of these terms will be useful for us in the remainder of this volume.

Gender assignment: A special case of gender attribution made just once—at birth—typically by a doctor or midwife. Usually, only the genitals are examined. The attending physician who at a birth shouts "It's a boy!" is performing "gender assignment."

Gender reassignment: A correction to a gender assignment "error," as in the case of intersex infants. Imagine that the doctor who shouted "It's a boy!" discovered on closer examination that the infant about whom she had made the initial gender attribution of male in fact had a partially fused vagina that resembled a scrotum and an enlarged clitoris resembling a penis. She would then confess to having made an error in the original gender attribution and would make a new gender attribution of female. This second, different, gender attribution is gender reassignment.

While Kessler and McKenna include "gender reassignment" in their lexicon of gender attribution terms, they prefer the term "gender reconstruction" in cases like the one described above because of the complexity of the decision process. They provocatively suggest that if "gender reassignment" is better termed "gender reconstruction," then perhaps "gender assignment" is better termed "gender construction." (We'll talk about some of the complexities surrounding gender reassignment/reconstruction in Chapter 7.) You should

---

6   Kessler and McKenna, 5–6.

note that gender reassignment is diagnostic, not surgical. Do not confuse it with surgical "sex reassignment."

Gender identity: The gender with which one identifies; that is—gender attribution performed on oneself. If I think of myself as female, that is my gender identity. Kessler and McKenna observe that the mechanisms for applying gender attribution to oneself are different from those for attributing gender to others. For instance, it is often held that self-gender-attribution occurs during a critical period. That is, it can't happen before a certain stage in one's life and can't be undone after that stage. Whatever the stage at which we perform self-gender attributions, we ourselves are the arbiters of our gender identities. Put differently, the only way to discern someone's gender identity is to ask that person.

Gender role: A set of prescriptions and proscriptions for behaviour based on one's gender. Kessler and McKenna distinguish gender roles from gender stereotypes since "stereotype" connotes an entrenched bias, whereas "role" is neutral. Gender roles can include the kinds of tasks people perform, their clothing and grooming practices, their status in society, and the kinds of virtues we attribute to them, among other things. Thus, for instance, some of the roles we associate with women in North America include nurturing others, and wearing make-up and skirts. By contrast, we sometimes associate North American men with such roles as occupying leadership positions and wearing suits and beards. While gender roles vary across cultures (women in North America wear pink, but pink is a manly colour in India), every culture assumes some gender roles.

Gender-role identity: How a person feels about and participates in the behaviours, feelings, etc. that are seen as appropriate for his/her gender. In one way or another, effeminate men and butch women both have gender-role identities that involve resisting prevailing gender norms. Similarly, women who object to being infantilized in professional settings and men who critique the taboo against male tears are unhappy with prevailing gender roles. Kessler and McKenna emphasize the importance of distinguishing gender identity from gender-role identity. Just because I'm ambivalent about the gender roles for women doesn't mean that I identify as a man.

2.4. "Sex" or "gender"?

We learned above that Kessler and McKenna use one word "gender" for both sex (the biological category) and gender (the category involving socio-cultural-psychological matters such as dress, behaviour, and identity). Let's finish this chapter by making explicit some reasons for and against distinguishing between the two terms.

Until well into the twentieth century, English speakers used the word "gender" solely as a grammatical term. If you speak French, for example, you know that all French nouns are either masculine (and take "*le*" or "*un*") or feminine (and take "*la*" or "*une*"). Some languages, like German and Russian, have three grammatical genders—masculine, feminine, and neuter. Back when "gender" was solely a grammatical term, English speakers used "sex" not only for the categories of male and female, but also for the categories of man and woman, and boy and girl.

Around the middle of the twentieth century, feminists sought to detach biological sex categories—which seemed to them fixed and inevitable—from the socio-cultural categories that seemed to emerge from those unchanging biological foundations. Famously, in 1949, the French philosopher Simone de Beauvoir asked "Are there even women?" Beauvoir wanted to know whether *woman* is a natural, unchanging, biological fact, or whether it is artifactual—a social construction like poetry or traffic laws. (We'll look more closely at Beauvoir's position in Chapter 4.) While Beauvoir and the mid-twentieth-century feminists who followed her regarded biological sex as natural, they regarded the gender roles—and indeed the genders—attendant upon biological sex as social constructions. Women, Beauvoir argued, are not born but *made* women.

There are two great advantages for the feminist of treating gender as distinct from sex. First, the expression of gender varies much more broadly over time and from place to place than sex traits do—this would be impossible if sex and gender were the very same thing.

The second advantage of treating sex and gender as distinct is practical, rather than empirical. For a long time, people thought of sex as fixed and inevitable. (Many people still think of it in this way.) So long as they thought of sex and gender as the same thing, this meant regarding gender too as fixed and inevitable. Detaching gender from sex opens the possibility that gender is not fixed and inevitable but rather fluid and changeable. This possibility has amazing liberatory potential. For example, once we regard gender as loose and contingent, there is no particular basis—at least no biological basis—for insisting that men are active, women are passive, and everyone is uncontroversially either a woman or a man for their whole lives. Thus, built in to the very concept of gender (as distinct from sex) is the notion of "gender bending"—the phenomenon of resisting gender norms.

We noted earlier that Kessler and McKenna opt to use the word "gender" for both the socio-cultural divisions between men and women, and masculine and feminine, and for the biological division between males and females, including the difference between male reproductive organs and female reproductive organs. Their stated reasons for doing this are threefold: (1) they wish to emphasize "that the element of social construction is primary in all aspects of being female or male;"[7] (2) they regard the distinction between sex and gender as "a technical one, applicable to scientists in the laboratory and some textbooks, but little else;"[8] and (3) they worry that in common usage most people flub the distinction between sex and gender, using both terms inconsistently and confusingly.

Among Kessler and McKenna's three reasons, the first has the most resonance with contemporary feminist theory. Since the 1990s, largely motivated by philosopher Judith Butler's pioneering work *Gender Trouble*, many feminist theorists have challenged the sex/gender distinction. On Butler's account, just as it makes sense to regard gender as malleable, contingent, and socially constructed, so also should we regard sex in this way. Butler argues that when we perform a Foucauldian genealogy of sex, we discover that the so-called biological facts about sex are "discursively produced by various scientific discourses in the service of other political and social interests."[9]

---

7   Kessler and McKenna, 7.
8   Kessler and McKenna, 7.
9   Judith Butler, *Gender Trouble: Feminism and the Subversion of Identity*, 7.

Social construction

To say that something is socially constructed is simply to say that it is the product of social forces. The practices of driving on the right in North America and on the left in the United Kingdom are socially constructed. While conventions for the operation of motor vehicles are obviously social in origin, much more interesting is the question of which human behaviours, categories, properties, and ideas are socially constructed, and which are part of the natural character of the species *homo sapiens*. Social constructivism is always more or less at odds with biodeterminism, the view that "biology is destiny." If you take the view that genetics entails that "men are men and women are women,"—that is, that one's gender-associated behaviour is a matter of genetics—then you are a biodeterminist about gender. If, on the other hand, you think that many women behave passively and that many men behave aggressively because both groups are socialized in these ways, then you are a social constructivist about (these alleged aspects of) gender.

What does it mean to be a social constructivist about sex? Put simply, social constructivists about sex regard the sex categories *male* and *female* (and the mechanisms whereby people and their parts are slotted into those categories) as reflecting prevailing social values rather than simply being a matter of underlying biological facts.

We'll look more closely at biodeterminism in Chapter 9 and at social constructivism in Chapter 12, but both ways of understanding sex and gender are threads that run through all of the discussions in this book.

We'll be hearing more about these complicated and difficult ideas in future chapters. For now, it's enough to say that for Butler, as well as for feminist philosophers, historians, sociologists, and biologists working in her tradition, biological sex markers are like the toe example from earlier in this chapter. That is, even though there may well be an objective fact of the matter regarding who has nine toes rather than ten or who has a penis rather than a vagina, we only pay special attention to the fact in question because we invest some practical, social importance in the number of toes or in the presence or absence of a penis. There are plenty of biological facts we never mention and others we choose to mention all the time.

Similarly, we make choices about which of these facts to mention together: we mention penises and XY chromosomes in the same contexts, but don't tend to discuss maximum heart rate in connection with penises and XY chromosomes, this despite the fact that certain maximum heart rates correlate more typically with people with XY chromosomes than with people with XX chromosomes. (We'll talk about maximum heart rates as they relate to sex in Chapter 4.) Arguably, there would be greater health benefit to most people in conjoining ideas about sex chromosomes with ideas about maximum heart-rate than with ideas about external genitalia. So, why don't we do so? Perhaps because the goals that are served by our clusters of sex concepts are primarily social rather than medical.

Philosopher Christine Overall offers a helpful elaboration of the view that biological sex is dependent upon gender norms:

> How do gender conventions construct sex identities? Feminists have identified three ways: first, by shaping individual bodies, through exercise, fashion and even surgery to make them conform to certain ideas of womanliness or manliness; second, by shaping entire groups of people, for example, through selective, gender-differentiated nutrition customs; and third, by identifying and recognizing certain bodily differences and configurations as significant of one's identity or essence.[10]

What are the practical consequences of taking the view that sex is socially constructed, just as gender is, and within the same system of power that gender is? Butler and Overall propose subtly different approaches.

For Butler, to regard sex as socially constructed, just as gender is, is to pull the biological rug out from under gender norms. When we see that the underpinnings of our ideas about both sex and gender

---

10   Christine Overall, "Return to Gender, Address Unknown: Reflections on the Past, Present, and Future of the Concept of Gender in Feminist Theory and Practice," 26.

are social, not biological, we can better envision the possibilities for alternative, liberatory gender norms. Overall is a bit more pessimistic. On her view, the very notion of gender is primarily oriented toward controlling and limiting people. We can no more liberate ourselves through alternative gender norms than we could through a different configuration of chains and locks. For this reason, she advocates the radical view that we should "junk" the idea of gender altogether. The result, she predicts, would be a more curious, more creative culture that resists hasty categorizations and places more emphasis on the specialness of individuals.[11]

This book concerns the metaphysics of sex and gender; so, clearly we haven't junked the idea of gender yet. Moreover, in this volume, we continue to distinguish between biological sex and socio-cultural gender in a way that Kessler and McKenna and Butler reject. We adopt this usage for the sake of clarity in order to conveniently disambiguate between different kinds of data and concepts. However, this stylistic choice should not invite complacency about the relationship between sex and gender. Keep your mind open, and as you continue to work through the volume, keep asking yourself what, if anything, the difference is between sex and gender.

2.5. Questions for reflection

- How much do you think our discourse is affected by systems of power? How effective do you think discursive analysis is in diagnosing the character of power in our society? In other societies? What sort of discursive practices around sex and gender as taxonomies can you think of? What kinds of systems of power might produce such discursive practices?
- Consider the ways in which various forms of discrimination and privilege intersect in your own identity. Do you identify with some of them more strongly than others?
- Is it possible to meet or interact with someone without performing a gender attribution? Have you ever done so?

---

11   Overall, 45.

- Which do you favour: maintaining the gender status quo, cultivating alternative genders (Butler) or junking the idea of gender altogether (Overall)? Why?

2.6. Works cited and recommended reading

Butler, Judith. *Gender Trouble: Feminism and the Subversion of Identity*. New York: Routledge, 1990.

Crenshaw, Kimberlé. "Demarginalizing the Intersection of Race and Sex: A Black Feminist Critique of Antidiscrimination Doctrine, Feminist Theory and Antiracist Politics." *The University of Chicago Legal Forum* 140 (1989): 139–67.

Foucault, Michel. *The History of Sexuality*. Vol. 1. Trans. Robert Hurley. New York: Random House, 1978.

Kessler, Suzanne and Wendy McKenna. *Gender: An Ethnomethodological Approach*. Brisbane: John Wiley and Sons, 1978.

Overall, Christine. "Return to Gender, Address Unknown: Reflections on the Past, Present, and Future of the Concept of Gender in Feminist Theory and Practice." *Marginal Groups and Mainstream American Culture*. Ed. Yolanda Estes, Arnold Farr, Patricia Smith, and Clelia Smyth. Lawrence: University Press of Kansas, 2000. 24–50.

CHAPTER 3

Aristotelian and Judeo-Christian Models of Sex Difference

3.1. Aristotle on the sexes

In this chapter, we consider two key arguments by the ancient Greek philosopher Aristotle (384–322 BCE), the first from *Metaphysics* and the second from *Generation of Animals*. By attending to these two classical texts, we can see that Aristotle gave considerable attention to biological sex taxonomies, and that he was inconsistent in his treatment of them.

Now, you might be asking yourself, why should we care what Aristotle thought about sex? While brilliant, Aristotle was wrong about a lot of things, and he's been dead for a long time. What difference does it make what he thought about sex? Understanding Aristotle's views on sex is important in part because doing so helps to reveal the ways our ideas about sex and gender vary from society to society and from era to era. However, these texts are not mere curiosities from the ancient world; they strongly influenced thought in the Jewish, Christian, and Muslim traditions. Medieval scholars from all three traditions drew upon Aristotelian thought, and its influence is still alive today.

3.1.1. Metaphysics (Book X, Ch. 9)

In Book X, Ch. 9 of the *Metaphysics*,[1] we find Aristotle's effort to explain how two things could be as different as males and females and yet belong to the same species.

Here is how Aristotle puts the question:

> One might raise the question, why woman does not differ from man in species, when female and male are contrary and their difference is a contrariety; and why a female and a male animal are not different in species, though this difference belongs to animal in virtue of its own nature, and not as paleness or darkness does; both "female" and "male" belong to it *qua* animal. This question is almost the same as the other, why one contrariety makes things different in species and another does not, e.g. "with feet" and "with wings" do, but paleness and darkness do not. Perhaps it is because the former are modifications peculiar to the genus, and the latter are less so. And since one element is definition and one is matter, contrarieties which are in the definition make a difference in species, but those which are in the thing taken as including its matter do not make one.[2]

Some key terms Aristotle uses

Elsewhere in the *Metaphysics*, Aristotle defines some key terms that you'll need in order to understand this section.

Essence: A thing's definition. What makes it the kind of thing that it is.

---

1   "Metaphysics" nowadays names the branch of philosophy concerned with the basic nature of reality. In Greek, the word "metaphysics" means "after physics," and it's likely that the compilation of Aristotle's works later called *Metaphysics* was so-called merely because it was usually presented in the curriculum after another work by Aristotle, the *Physics*.

2   Aristotle, *Metaphysics* X.9, in *The Basic Works of Aristotle*, 848.

Essential property: A property that makes a thing the kind of thing that it is. If that property were missing, the object in question would be a different kind of thing. For example, Aristotle regards the capacity for rationality as essential to human beings. Anything that lacks the capacity for rationality must be something other than a human being.

Accident (or accidental property): A property that doesn't make any difference to the kind of thing something is. It doesn't matter whether a horse is white, grey, or brown. It is still a horse. Changing its colour doesn't change the kind of thing that it is. Thus, its colour is merely an accident. (Note: this is distinct from, although related to, our contemporary usage of "accident" to mean something done not on purpose.)

Form/matter: Matter is the stuff something is made of. Form is, roughly, the thing's structure. On Aristotle's account, every individual thing is "enformed matter." That is, it's made up of some kind of stuff (matter), assembled in a particular way (form). Form isn't just shape, though. It is, more broadly, what a thing is like. If a being is rational, then that is part of its form. The very same matter that makes it up could in principle have gone into the make-up of a non-rational being. In that sense, matter is more malleable and versatile than form. On Aristotle's account, form and matter always come as a package. Unformed matter does not exist, nor does matterless form.

Contrariety: Two properties that cannot coexist at the same time (in the same respect) in the same thing. *Alive* and *dead* are contrarieties since the very same thing cannot at once be both alive and dead.

Qua: Considered as. "Qua" is a useful little adverb that allows Aristotle to draw his readers' attention to just one aspect of a thing that has multiple aspects. For instance, we might consider a woman qua female, qua animal, or qua human being. *Qua* female, woman has a certain reproductive function. *Qua* animal, she has certain sensory and metabolic capacities. *Qua* human being, she has a certain rational capacity.

According to Aristotle, contrarieties are used to distinguish between different species. One such contrariety is *winged* vs. *wingless*. An individual cannot be both with wings and without wings since these are contrarieties. When contrarieties span entire classes of things, they serve to individuate between species. That is, if one animal has wings and another does not, the fact that they are contrary in this way tells you that they belong to different species.

The male/female contrariety is a special problem for Aristotle. On the one hand, this contrariety, as with winged/not winged, does distinguish between two large groups. However, Aristotle is committed to the view that males and females coexist within the same species and, thus, that the male/female contrariety does not differentiate them as separate species. One of his chief reasons for denying that males and females are separate species derives from facts about reproduction. At the end of his *Metaphysics* discussion of sex, he observes that "the same seed becomes female or male by being acted on in a certain way." Essentially, the fact that the same individual can produce both male and female offspring obliges Aristotle to regard males and females as belonging to the same species, and he knows his metaphysics needs to make sense of this fact

Here is his simple solution: There are contrarieties of form. These are differences in a thing's essential properties. If two things have contrarieties of form, they have different definitions and thus constitute different species. (*With wings* and *without wings* is such a contrariety.) However, there are also contrarieties of matter. These are differences in a thing's accidental properties and make no difference to which species things belong. Pale and dark are such contrarieties. While the very same thing cannot be both pale and dark at the same time, whether a thing is pale or dark makes no difference to what kind of thing it is.

Form and matter

The foundation of Aristotle's metaphysics is hylomorphism—his view that every existing thing is made up of both form and matter, and that form and matter are inseparable. Some examples will help to illustrate the basics of this view.

On Aristotle's account, two different statues of Napoleon, both cast from the same mold, share the same form. While they share one form, they are nonetheless two statues, not one. The reason for this can be found in their matter. Two quantities of matter entail two things, even if they share one form.

Aristotle thinks that the two statues cast from the same mold share the same form regardless of what kind of matter they're composed of. Just as two brass statues of Napoleon share a single form, so does a brass statue and a plaster one. Regardless of whether the statues are composed of marble or plaster or something else altogether, they are statues because of their form. For Aristotle, it is form, not matter, that tells you what kind of a thing you are dealing with. Brass, wooden, and porcelain bowls are all bowls, irrespective of their material. Conversely, a brass statue and a brass bowl are different kinds of things, even though they're composed of the same matter.

In summary, then, form determines the kind of thing, while matter determines the quantity of things. Two different forms entail two different kinds of thing; two quantities of matter entail two things (but not necessarily two kinds of thing—*that* depends on how many forms are involved).

It is easy to see how Aristotle's form/matter distinction maps on to his essence/accident distinction. While a thing's form is essential to it—i.e., makes it the kind of thing that it is—its matter is accidental and does not affect the kind of thing that it is. If a wooden bowl were petrified and turned to stone, it would remain a bowl since its essence would remain unchanged even though one of its accidental properties had undergone a dramatic change.

Aristotle argues that male/female is just such a contrariety—a difference of matter, not form. Thus, metaphysically, there is, for Aristotle, no more difference between a man and a woman than between a pale man and a dark man.

3.1.2. Generation of Animals (Book IV)

Generation of Animals is Aristotle's account of sexual reproduction. According to Aristotle, the male/female distinction occurs in all species of plants and animals. They are separate in the "most perfect of them." Thus, for instance, most flowering plants, being less perfect than mammals, contain both male and female organs in the very same individual. The problem that Aristotle seeks to solve in *Generation of Animals* is how sexual reproduction is able to produce separate sexes to begin with.

Remember Aristotle's notion of form, the as-it-were blueprint for individual things? At the most basic level, Aristotle thinks that new individual things come to be when matter is enformed differently—that is, when it is rearranged from whatever form it used to take according to a new (to it) "blueprint." The trouble is that, as we saw in *Metaphysics* X.9, Aristotle maintains that males and females of the same species share the same form; they only differ in matter. And yet, we see consistent sex-based differences within species. In *Generation of Animals*, Aristotle seeks to explain how, despite a common essence, males and females within species manifest such striking differences.

Before Aristotle offers his own explanation of the reproductive origin of separate sexes, he first surveys other ancient scholars' attempts to answer this question. He summarizes three different explanations for sexual difference:

1. Anaxagoras argues that males and females simply derive from different types of sperm. He seems to imply that the right testicle produces males and the left testicle produces females.
2. By contrast, Empedocles argues that all sperm are the same until they enter the womb, whereupon the temperature of the womb determines the sex of the offspring—a cold womb results in a female and a warm womb results in a male.
3. Finally, Democritus of Abdera agrees with Empedocles that sex differences develop in utero. However, he denies that the temperature of the womb can explain the difference. Rather, he describes a kind of battle between male and female reproductive fluid in which one "prevails" over the other. If the male reproductive fluid prevails, the offspring will be male; if the female reproductive fluid prevails, the offspring will be female.

Aristotle agrees with Empedocles and Democritus of Abdera that sex is determined in utero. Like Empedocles, he thinks that heat has something to do with it, but he thinks that Empedocles's account is too simplistic. After all, argues Aristotle, male and female twins are produced at the same time in the same womb. If the only factor determining sex were the temperature of the womb, this would be impossible.

In his own answer to the puzzle, he retains Empedocles's emphasis on heat, but builds in Democritus's notion of "prevailing" for a richer, more complex account of pre-natal sexual development.

For Aristotle, the fact that males and females possess the same essence or form entails that their (males' and females') structure and function is similar. On his view, female sex organs may differ superficially from male sex organs, but they are ultimately just two expressions of the very same structure. He similarly regards male and female sex organs as functioning in the same way, despite superficial differences. For Aristotle, the difference between males and females is not form or function but ability. In particular, he regards males as able to produce reproductive fluid containing form, and females as unable to do so. (We will return to this historical account of females as "underperforming males" in Chapter 10.)

Female semen

We have been using the phrase "reproductive fluid" here, but in fact both Democritus of Abdera and Aristotle refer to both male and female *semen*. What is going on here? In fact, it wasn't until the seventeenth century that scientists realized that mammals produced eggs. While ancient scientists were of course aware of bird eggs, they regarded them as mere vessels, and not as themselves containing what we would today term genetic material. (The concept of genetics was not available to Aristotle or Democritus.) Unaware that mammals produce eggs, many ancient thinkers took the view that both male and female mammals produce semen. Of course, this hypothesis aligns well with Aristotle's view that males and females perform the very same reproductive functions, but with different degrees of proficiency. (For a great, highly readable account of the history of the science of sex, see Matthew Cobb,

Generation: The Seventeenth-Century Scientists Who Unraveled the Secrets of Sex, Life, and Growth [New York: Bloomsbury, 2006].)

Aristotle terms the production of reproductive fluid "concoction." Concoction in this sense is rather like distillation. We begin with unconcocted blood, and use our physical heat to distill it down into reproductive fluid. Aristotle argues that without sufficient heat in the concoction process, the resulting reproductive fluid would be incapable of transmitting the form of the parent. It is perhaps unsurprising to learn that Aristotle considers only males capable of generating sufficient physical heat to concoct blood into form-bearing semen.

Who's hot and who's not?

Of course, Aristotle did not have thermometers available to him. So, what was his basis for arguing that men are hotter than women? Again, it is useful to think of distillation. A hotter still causes more water to evaporate, leading to a more intense reduction. (If you've ever made soup stock or balsamic reduction or maple syrup, you will be familiar with this principle.) Aristotle argued that since women bleed for about a week every month, they must be overflowing with too much blood; this shows that their bodies are not hot enough to concoct that blood as well as men do.

Today, the view espoused by both Empedocles and Aristotle that temperature determines sex sounds quite far-fetched. However, this is exactly how sex differentiation occurs in many reptile species. In those species, the gestational temperature during a critical developmental period determines the sex of the embryo. So, it turns out that Empedocles and Aristotle were quite right to suggest that heat can be a mechanism for sex differentiation. They were just wrong to think that it applies to all dimorphic species. In particular, they were wrong to think that human sexual differentiation occurs in this way.

For Aristotle, offspring who resemble the male parent are the result of the father's excellent concoction of reproductive fluid. The formal principle is perfectly present in his semen; hence, it easily prevails over the matter in the female reproductive fluid, enforming it with the father's essence. However, just as females concoct less well than males, some males concoct less well than others, and some males concoct more perfectly on some occasions than on others. When the male reproductive fluid is less perfectly concocted, it is less successful at prevailing over and hence enforming the female reproductive fluid. In such cases, the father's essence will be only imperfectly transmitted to the offspring. For Aristotle, this failure to prevail results in female offspring, but also in disabled offspring, and in general in any failure to resemble the father. Notice, however, that these imperfections are not themselves new forms; instead, they reflect formal deficiencies. Thus, the disabled male parent might nonetheless concoct his reproductive fluid well enough for it to prevail perfectly over the female. In this case, his offspring would not be disabled.

Of course, we now know that, in many species, the offspring's sex really is determined by the male parent. In humans, for instance, the female parent contributes an X-chromosome to the offspring's sex chromosome pair. It is the X or Y contributed by the male parent that determines the offspring's sex. Where Aristotle went wrong was in thinking that all other physical features the offspring inherits are also furnished by the male parent.

The female as monster

The great medieval theologian/philosopher St. Thomas Aquinas was deeply influenced by Aristotle, and by Aristotle's account of sex differentiation. Following Aristotle, Aquinas declares that

> the active principle in the male seed always tends toward the generation of a male offspring, which is more perfect than the female. From this it follows that conception of female offspring is something of an accident in the order of nature—in so far, at least, as it is not the result of the natural causality of the particular agent. Therefore, if there were no other natural influence at work tending toward the conception of female offspring, such conception would be wholly outside the design of nature, as is the case with what we call "monstrous" births.[3]

---

3   St. Thomas Aquinas, *The Disputed Questions on Truth*, Vol. 1. Qu. 5, art. 9, d. 9, in *The Collected Works of St. Thomas Aquinas*, 245.

Medieval thinkers thought of all birth defects as monstrosities, in the sense of two-headed calves or dog-headed people. Inspired by Aristotle, medievals attributed such monstrosities to a failure by the form communicated in the father's semen to shape the matter contained in the female reproductive fluid. On Aquinas's account, what distinguished the birth of females from the birth of other monsters was God's will that nature contain both males and females. Thus, while he regarded the generation of individual females as accidental (in the strict Aristotelian sense), he thought that the consistent accidental generation of females was part of God's plan for a well-ordered universe.

At the outset of this chapter, I remarked that Aristotle's treatment of biological sex involved a philosophical inconsistency. It should now be apparent where that inconsistency resides. Recall that, for the Aristotle of *Metaphysics* X.9, males and females share the very same form and only differ in matter. Recall also that, for Aristotle, there is no matter without form. Nonetheless, in *Generation of Animals*, we find Aristotle arguing that females are deficient in form and, in particular, that female reproductive fluid is formless matter. Thus, Aristotle's account of sexual reproduction, while more sophisticated than his contemporaries', arguably comes at the cost of his core metaphysical principles.

Aristotle and contemporary feminist scholarship

You might think that contemporary feminist scholars would take little interest in what Aristotle thought about sex difference. In fact, some important recent scholarship on gender takes its lead from Aristotle. Philosopher Marguerite Deslauriers, for instance, works on gender in Plato and Aristotle. In her research on Aristotle, she praises Aristotle's account of sex difference in the *Metaphysics* but argues that Aristotle's sexist biases creep into his discussion of sex and gender in *Generation of Animals* and *The Politics*. Philosopher Charlotte Witt, by contrast, draws on Aristotle to develop her own distinctive "gender uniessentialism"—roughly, her view that gender is a functional essence that is constitutive of each of us as individuals. Put more simply, for Witt, gender is a principle that organizes and unifies each of us as social individuals.

3.2. Biblical and theological accounts of sex

If you had to summarize the account of creation in the first two chapters of the Bible, it might go something like this: Over the course of six days, God creates the earth, and then vegetation, then animals of various kinds, then, in His own image, men and women to rule over the other living creatures. He sees that it is very good. Then he makes the earth (again!), and then streams (but not yet any plants). He makes a man out of dust and places him in the Garden of Eden, where He creates plants, and lots of other nice things. God assigns the man to care for the garden. God sees that the man needs a helper. One after another, He brings to the man various wild animals. The man (now called Adam) names the animals, but none of them turns out to be a suitable helper. So, God puts Adam to sleep, removes one of his ribs and fashions a woman out of the rib. He brings her to Adam, who names her.

When you read Genesis 1 and 2, you cannot escape the impression that what we actually have are two creation accounts. In the two chapters, we get two similar but not quite identical descriptions of God's creation of the earth. What is similar about them? Well, they list similar sorts of created things—earth, sky, water, plants, animals....

More striking, however, is the differences between them. First of all, the two accounts have God creating things in a different order. Most notably, in the first account, He creates plants and animals before he creates human beings, and He creates men and women at the same time. In the second account, God seems to create Adam first, then plants, then animals, then Eve. What other differences are there? Well, in Genesis 1, we hear about the form for human beings—they are made in God's image—but we hear nothing about the material from which they are made. In Genesis 2, by contrast, there is no mention of the form for human beings; only the material of which they are made—dust in Adam's case, a rib in Eve's—is mentioned. Finally, the two accounts have men and women playing different roles. In Genesis 1, men and women are both, it seems, intended to be caretakers of the other creatures. In Genesis 2, Adam is assigned the task of caretaker for the Garden of Eden; later, Eve is designated as his helper. Moreover, in Genesis 2 (but not in Genesis 1), God has Adam name non-human animals and, of course, Eve.

The power of naming

As we have seen, in Genesis 2, Adam names the animals and Eve. Notice the symbolic force of this fact. To be in a position to name someone or something usually means that the namer occupies a position of relative power. Who gets to name someone or something? Parents. Owners. Inventors. Colonizers. Sovereigns. What does it say about Adam's relationship with Eve and the animals that he is the one who names them? What does it say about Eve that she does not name anyone or anything?

What could possibly explain this difference between Genesis 1 and Genesis 2? One superficial reading might be that God created the world twice. Indeed, sometimes, one hears accounts that the woman made, like the man, in God's image in Genesis 1 was Adam's alleged first wife, Lilith. (Lilith occurs in legend and in Hebrew Apocrypha.) However, the more likely explanation is quite simply that Genesis 1 and 2 were two separate creation stories, composed at different times, and later combined. The so-called "Documentary Hypothesis" (sometimes termed the "Graf-Wellhausen Hypothesis," after Karl Heinrich Graf and Julius Wellhausen, the two nineteenth-century German biblical scholars who pioneered the approach) says that the Torah was composed in just this way.

While the Documentary Account is not necessarily committed to a particular number of separate strands in the Torah, the Graf-Wellhausen Hypothesis, and versions of the Documentary Hypothesis that hew closely to it, identifies four main strands:

- J (Jahwist), c. 950 BCE
- E (Elohist), c. 850 BCE
- D (Deuteronomist), c. 621 BCE
- P (Priestly), c. 450 BCE

The two that are of particular interest to us in Genesis 1 and 2 are the J and P strands.

The Torah, or Pentateuch, comprises the first five books of the Hebrew Bible (that is, of what the Christians call the Old Testament):

- B'reshit (Genesis)
- Sh'mot (Exodus)
- Vayyikra (Leviticus)
- Bemidbar (Numbers)
- D'varim (Deuteronomy)

The J-strand is so-named because the name most often used for God in that strand is Yahweh (or, in Graf and Wellhausen's German, '*Jahweh*'). The oldest of the four strands, the J-strand is the product of an ancient, nomadic culture, whose religion still retains elements of regional myths and legends. The God of the J-strand is personal—He speaks with his subjects, loves some of them, gets angry at others of them, and is occasionally prone to error. Produced five centuries later, the P-strand is the product of a settled, agrarian people with a long-established priesthood and set of laws. Where the J-strand includes the kind of vivid and engaging stories that one might tell around the fire, the P-strand reflects the sophisticated philosophical thought of a mature priestly caste. The God of the P-strand is more abstract and perfect, and consequently less personal, than the God of the J-strand.

Let's review the main features of the two creation stories. In Genesis 1, God creates the world in an orderly way from the simplest to the most complex beings (according to our usual conception of the comparative complexity of species)—plants, then animals, then human beings—and he gets it right the first time: "It was very good." In Genesis 2, the order of creation is more idiosyncratic: God creates plants and Adam around the same time because He needs Adam to tend the plants. Adam himself needs help—something God didn't seem to anticipate when He first created him. So, God creates a series of animals as possible helpers, and only afterwards resorts to the creation of Eve. Compared to the Genesis 1 account, this one is strikingly *ad hoc*. God doesn't get things right initially; so, he keeps plugging away at it.

In Genesis 1, the form of human beings (in the image of God) is evidently more important than their matter. Genesis 2, by contrast, is silent on the human form, but attends to the material of which humans are made. This, especially the use of the rib to create Eve, suggests that God has to make do with the materials He has on hand.

Genesis 1 is much more egalitarian than Genesis 2, with both men and women made in God's image and charged with the care of the non-human animals. By contrast, Genesis 2 clearly places Adam in a position of authority over Eve. Not only is he created first, but she is created specifically in order to assist him. Moreover, Adam names her, just as he does the other animals.

Given these clear contrasts, it is perhaps unsurprising to learn that, according to the Graf-Wellhausen Hypothesis, the creation story that occurs in Genesis 2 is the older of the two. It belongs to the J-strand, allegedly composed around 950 BCE. By contrast, the philosophical sophistication of the Genesis 1 account marks it as part of 450 BCE P-strand.

So, while some people draw many of their views about the natures and roles of men and women, and of the differences between them, from religious texts, even this very brief snapshot from the Bible (and, hence, from Judeo-Christianity) shows that religious texts themselves are influenced by the cultures in which they are produced.

3.3. St. Augustine: A medieval Christian interpretation

While nowadays the "seams" between the different texts in the Bible appear obvious, until around the seventeenth century most Jewish and Christian scholars thought that Moses wrote the whole Torah, as given to him by God.[4] They were thus unable to explain inconsistencies in the text as the result of different authors writing in different historical contexts. Thus, we find pre-seventeenth-century

---

4   While rabbinical scholars generally agree that God gave the Torah to Moses, they debate when He did this, and whether He did it all at once or over several intervals.

theologians (and some post seventeenth-century ones) seeking philo-sophical and theological mechanisms to reconcile apparent incon-sistencies. Among those who sought to reconcile the inconsistencies between Genesis 1 and Genesis 2 was philosopher and theologian St. Augustine of Hippo (354–430 CE).

In a short text from his *De Trinitate* (*On the Trinity*), Augustine attempts to reconcile the Apostle Paul's advice to the Corinthians that women should cover their heads with the Genesis 1 creation account. Paul argues that men must not cover their heads since they are made in God's image. However, he argues that woman is made from man, and hence is a reflection not of God but of man. As such, she must cover her head. Clearly, Paul's policy for men derives from Genesis 1 while his policy for women comes from Genesis 2. Augustine discerns that Genesis 1 should also apply to women, and attempts to defend Paul's position while respecting the claim in Genesis 1 that woman, like man, is made in God's image.

Augustine argues that human beings are made in God's image not in some bodily sense, but in the sense that they share in God's ratio-nality. That is, we are made in God's image not because of what we look like but because we, like God, are capable of reason. According to Augustine, this is true of both men and women, and hence both men and women are recipients of God's grace. However, he argues, we are most like God when we use our intellect to contemplate the higher, eternal things, rather than the lower, quotidian ones.

According to Augustine, women's particular bodily nature more naturally disposes them than men to attend to lower, day-to-day matters. This leads to a natural division of labour in which women think about the baser things, thereby freeing men up to attend to more elevated ideas. It is in this sense, argues Augustine, that woman is a helper or "help-meet" to man.

This notion of a sort of rational division of labour actually dates back to Aristotle, who argues that the higher species are divided into sexes for precisely this reason. Indeed, the idea that the human essential property of rationality is best exemplified by men due to just such a sexual division of labour is bound up with Aristotle's view that only male parents are able to communicate form or essence to their offspring.

Temporal versus eternal things

Augustine concludes the chapter by attributing to women "the government of temporal things"—that is, things that are worldly, physical, practical, secular—and to men "the beholding or the consulting of the eternal reasons of things."[5] Notice the fascinating division of labour that emerges here. What might the practical consequences look like? Grocery lists and household finances for women? Math and logic for men? We'll come back to this way of thinking in Chapter 11, where we will learn that Rousseau's instructions for the differential education of boys and girls reproduces precisely this division of labour.

Like Aristotle, Augustine regards men and women as differing in matter not form, but regards men as better exemplifying that form than women. Thus, argues Augustine, as a member of the human species, woman is characterized by rationality, and hence reflects God's image. However, since her body disposes her to attend to worldly matters, whereas men are apparently unencumbered (or less encumbered) by such concerns, woman does not exemplify God's image as perfectly as man does. Thus, on her own—that is, considered strictly as a woman—she does not reflect God. She is, instead, a reflection of man. As such, she is enjoined to be humble and to cover her head, unlike man who, as a direct reflection of God, is prohibited from doing so. (In Chapter 11, we will revisit this idea that woman is a reflection of man, not God.)

Here is how Augustine puts the matter:

> [T]he woman together with her own husband is the image of God, so that that whole substance may be one image; but when she is referred separately to her quality of *help-meet*, which regards the woman herself alone, then she is not the image of God; but as regards the man alone, he is the image of God as fully and completely as when the woman too is joined with him in one.[6]

---

5   St. Augustine, *On the Trinity*, Book XII, Chapter VII, in *Basic Writings of St. Augustine*, Vol. 2, 816.

6   St. Augustine, 814.

Put simply, for Augustine man reflects the image of God whether he is on his own or in union with his wife. Woman, on the other hand, reflects the image of God when she is in union with her husband, but not when she is considered in her own right.

Still today in many churches around the world, men remove their hats and women wear hats or veils. If ever you see such a congregation, remember that within those norms for attire lurk a tension spanning ancient Greek philosophy, two distinct periods within Judaism, two other periods in Christianity, and some 13 centuries.

3.4. Questions for reflection

- Aristotle thinks that it is the *differences* between male parents and their offspring, rather than the similarities between them, that require explanation. Why do you think that difference is harder for him to account for than similarity? In general, do you think that scientists and other scholars are more puzzled by difference or by similarity? Can you think of examples from other fields that illustrate this?
- Consider the evidence about sexual reproduction that is available without modern instruments such as thermometers and microscopes. Can you imagine a different explanatory account of that evidence than the one Aristotle developed? Can you imagine one in which the female is not deficient?
- How great a role do you think religious texts play within society? How great a role do you think our cultures play in our understanding of religious texts?
- Augustine states but neither explains nor defends the idea that a woman's bodily nature better suits her to attend to lower matters than to higher ones. What do you think he has in mind? What defence for this view might he offer if pressed?
- Are you familiar with a religious tradition besides the two discussed in this chapter? Are there tensions like the ones described above in texts of that faith? What are the respective roles of men and women within that tradition?

3.5. Works cited and recommended reading

Aquinas, Saint Thomas. *The Disputed Questions on Truth*. Vol.
1. Qu. 5, art. 9, d. 9. *The Collected Works of St. Thomas
Aquinas*, electronic edition. Charlottesville: Intelex, 1993.
Aristotle. Book X, Chapter 9. *Metaphysics*. *The Basic Works of
Aristotle*. Ed. Richard McKeon. New York: Random House,
1941.
———. *Generation of Animals*. Trans. A.L. Peck. London:
Heinemann, 1943.
Augustine, Saint. *On the Trinity*. Book XII, Chapter VII. *Basic
Writings of Saint Augustine*. Vol. 2. Ed. W.J. Oates. New
York: Random House, 1948.
Cobb, Matthew. *Generation: The Seventeenth-Century Scientists
Who Unraveled the Secrets of Sex, Life, and Growth*. New
York: Bloomsbury, 2006.
Deslauriers, Marguerite. "Sex Difference and Essence in
Aristotle's Metaphysics and Biology." *Feminist Interpretations
of Aristotle*. Ed. Cynthia Freeland. University Park:
Pennsylvania State University Press, 1998. 138–67.
Genesis 1–2. *The New English Bible*. Cambridge: Cambridge
University Press, 1970.
Witt, Charlotte. *The Metaphysics of Gender*. Oxford: Oxford
University Press, 2011.

CHAPTER 4

The Second Sex

4.1. The default setting

Is there a "standard" of human being—an archetype that we picture when we think of people? With all of the variety in the human species, you wouldn't think so. However, some of our linguistic practices suggest that, in general, when we think of human beings, we think of men.

If a friend invited you to a hockey game, for instance, you might well be surprised to get there and find that the players were women. Lots of people still use "hockey" to refer to men's hockey and "women's hockey" to refer to women's hockey. Similarly, while such practices are becoming less common, you might still have a grandparent who distinguishes between "doctors" and "lady doctors," or between "bus drivers" and "woman bus drivers." Of course, some of these assumptions are loosely based on statistics. Overall, hockey players are still today much more likely to be male than female. On the other hand, phrases like "lady doctor" persist despite the fact that 33 per cent of US physicians, 40 per cent of Canadian physicians, and about half of students in most North American medical schools, are women.

We find related phenomena in the health sciences, where it is still common for researchers to study a sample of male subjects and simply extrapolate the results to females. For instance, until 2010, health researchers recommended using the very same formula to calculate maximum heart rates for men and women. The formula was derived from empirical studies on male subjects; researchers assumed that, since the cardiovascular system isn't "sexual," the same formula would work for women. In 2010, however, a Northwestern Medicine study[1] of 5500 healthy women showed that women's maximum heart rates were actually lower than men's. It turns out that the exercise advice women had been receiving for decades was not only wrong but dangerous.

> For a great, up-to-date resource on the science of gender, sex and health, check out the Canadian Institutes of Health Research — Institute of Gender and Health's *What a Difference Sex and Gender Make: A Gender, Sex and Health Research Casebook* at <http://www.cihr-irsc.gc.ca/e/44734.html>.

Many engineers and designers have also historically treated males as the "default setting" for the whole species. This made the news in 2008 when the United States Transportation Department issued new rules that, starting with the 2010 model year, automotive manufacturers must begin using smaller "female" crash test dummies in addition to the standard male dummies to test car safety.[2] Prior to this decision, smaller dummies were used for testing, but only in the back seats because they were taken to represent children. The new rules stipulate that 4'8" 108 pound dummies must be tested in the front passenger seat. Old habits die hard, however—the new rules don't oblige safety testers to put these smaller dummies in the driver's seat.

In this chapter, we examine three different takes on this tendency to think of males as "standard" humans and females as a

---

1   Martha Gulati and Henry R. Black, "Heart Rate Response to Exercise Stress Testing in Asymptomatic Women: The St. James Women Take Heart Project," 130–37.

2   Jordan Weissmann, "Female Crash Dummies Part of Updated Vehicle Safety Tests," *The Washington Post*, 9 July 2008.

kind of "special case." In the first of these, existentialist philosopher Simone de Beauvoir argues that, historically, women have been constructed as "the Other" to men's "One." Next, we'll look at psychoanalyst Sigmund Freud's late attempts to understand the female as not-male. The chapter concludes with Luce Irigaray's efforts to stand Freud on his head, and, with him, the "othering" of woman.

4.2. Beauvoir: Woman as the "Other"

On the first page of her *The Second Sex* (first published in French in 1949) philosopher Simone de Beauvoir poses a striking question: "Are there even women?"[3] The question seems, at first, an odd one. Of course there are women. We see them all around us. However, Beauvoir is concerned to discover not just whether there *are* women (a question easily enough answered) but whether there are women *really*. To better understand what this means, we will need to take a short detour into metaphysics.

One of the main occupations of metaphysicians is to theorize about what really exists in the world—that is, what exists in fact and not merely in language or in our minds. The question of what sorts of things really exist was one that in particular occupied medieval philosophers, who energetically debated the question of whether only individual things (like this horse or that horse) are real, or whether the broad types which the individuals exemplify (e.g., horse as type or species) are real too.

We all know what we're seeing when we see an individual example of the horse type (i.e., when we see an individual horse), but is the type *horse* something over and above the individual examples? Those who considered types to be real were termed "realists." By contrast, the "nominalists" claimed that only individual things count as real, and that the terms we use for types of things are mere conveniences of speech that do not pick out any real entities in the world. (Notice that "nominalism" contains as

---

3   Simone de Beauvoir, *The Second Sex*, 3. For many years, the standard
      English version of *The Second Sex* famously translated this question as
      "Are there women really?" While the now authoritative 2011 translation
      translates the question differently, the spirit remains the same.

its stem the French word "*nom*" derived from the Latin "nomen," both meaning *name*.)

Even as she questions the reality of womanhood as a type, Beauvoir concedes that "nominalism is a doctrine that falls a bit short; and it is easy for antifeminists to show that women *are* not men."[4] In claiming that nominalism "falls a bit short," Beauvoir perhaps means to allow that some types—like horse, for example, and not just individual examples like Secretariat and Northern Dancer—are real. However, she further implies that this kind of realism has its dangers. In particular, "antifeminists" often embrace a realist point of view when they claim a categorical distinction between men and women, and Beauvoir herself is skeptical that the realist perspective can be extended unproblematically to the category of woman. In effect, she raises the possibility that even though some general terms pick out real types, other such terms may be less straightforward, the term "woman" being a case in point. (Recall that we encountered in Chapter 1 in Borges's "certain Chinese encyclopedia" the notion that some general terms are more controversial than others.)

On Beauvoir's account, the telltale sign that "woman" is not a natural kind term like "horse" is that we are "exhorted to be women, stay women, become women."[5] No one would think to urge a horse to be a horse, remain a horse, or become a horse. No one worries that a horse might at some stage not really be a horse anymore, but we occasionally do hear such worries about women. If females can stop being women, if they need to remain women by some kind of active exertion, then this would suggest that they are not naturally women—that someone must be raised to be a woman just as one must be trained to be a violinist, and that they must be raised or trained to cooperate in this endeavour.

Beauvoir's question "Are there even women?" is of crucial histori-cal importance in gender studies not only because it invites us to re-examine whether womanhood is natural or artifactual, but also because it opens the door to similar critical questions about gender.

4   Beauvoir, 4.
5   Beauvoir, 3.

The Second Sex   51

As you work through the material in this volume, reflect on the following questions:

- Are there even men and women?
- Are there even males and females?
- Are there even sexes?

Woman, it seems, is a more mysterious and complex concept than just "adult female human." As Beauvoir tries to make sense of woman, she considers and rejects a number of accounts of what the word means. She mocks the idea that woman is a timeless essence; the very idea, she says, is vague and ultimately meaningless. She rejects the notion that women share a feminine essence on the same grounds that, she says, the social and biological sciences reject the reality of racial essences.

However, Beauvoir is also critical of those who would reject womanhood altogether. Too often, she argues, those women who just want to be treated as human beings are in fact emulating not human beings in general but men in particular. Indeed, she suggests that some of these women are only able to adopt such post-feminine roles through the influence of the powerful men in their lives.

On Beauvoir's account, the very fact that we can ask the question: "What is a woman?" provides some hint about the nature of womanhood. No one would ask such a question about men. While maleness is taken for granted as the norm, women must identify themselves as women (recall our "lady doctor" and "women's hockey," above).

"Woman" and "man" are not symmetrical terms, continues Beauvoir. They are best understood not as two poles, but rather as a centre and a bias. The masculine is regarded as the absolute, neutral human type, while femininity is regarded as a kind of peculiarity— a deviation from the norm. Put simply, Beauvoir argues, we treat man as the One and woman as the Other. Beauvoir argues that the Other is a primordial category. "No group ever defines itself as One without immediately setting up the Other opposite itself," she writes.[6] On her account, we do this automatically, unthinkingly. If

---

6   Beauvoir, 6.

three strangers share a train car, they naturally start feeling more connection with each other, and feeling a vague hostility towards the occupants of the other cars. We form our various identities by contrasting them with an Other. The Other is, on Beauvoir's account, a necessary but fluid category. As history chugs along, as wars are won and lost, as groups migrate to different parts of the world, exactly who counts as the Other changes. Make no mistake, though—someone is Othered, even if it is not always the same someone.

> Beauvoir maintains that the One/Other distinction does not origi-
> nate with males and females in particular. However, some feminists
> disagree on this point. Turn to Chapter 9 to see Marxist feminist
> Shulamith Firestone's dissenting take on the primordial nature of
> the distinction.

Woman is the exception to this rule. Always and everywhere, woman has been the Other, says Beauvoir. Often, such long-term dominance of one category by another can be traced back to numbers, but women are not a minority. In cases of the oppression of minorities, generally the oppression is an historical accident. Hence, the oppressed retain the memory of former days before they were oppressed. There are no such former days for women.

Beauvoir, heavily influenced by mid-twentieth-century French Marxism, compares women to the Proletariat. Neither women nor the Proletariat constitute a minority and yet both are "Othered" by "the One" and neither group can look back to a history prior to their Othering since both have been Othered for as long as they have existed. However, whereas the Proletariat has not always existed, there have always been women. Moreover, unlike the Proletariat, women cannot even dream of abolishing the ruling class; there will always be men.

The other key difference between women and the Proletariat that Beauvoir identifies is that members of the Proletariat work shoulder to shoulder on factory floors and hence are able to organize and to develop a group identity. By contrast, women are isolated within the private sphere, living beside not other women, but men. This dissipation of women blocks female solidarity; it prevents women from identifying with other women. As a consequence, argues Beauvoir, women, unlike Proletarians, have no "We."

Beauvoir compares women to the Proletariat. Whom exactly does she have in mind? "Proletariat" is the term used by Marxists to refer to the large urban working class, the members of which worked the factories that came into existence with the Industrial Revolution. Like women, they are not a minority, and like women—but unlike an ethnic or religious minority—they did not exist independently before coming into relation with the ruling classes. However, unlike women, they have not always existed (and hence, unlike women, have not always existed as Other). There was no Proletariat before the Industrial Revolution.

The consequent intractability of women's Othering means that many people regard women's subordinate position as natural, even perhaps necessary. For Beauvoir, nature is not necessity; change is possible. However, she warns that the kind of change toward which women should strive ought not to be confused with happiness. Too often, she writes, happiness is confused with being at rest. To think of happiness in this way, indeed to seek to measure the happiness of others, serves those who wish to impose a particular situation on those others. Beauvoir argues that we cannot really know what happiness means.

The only appropriate goal for a human being, she argues, is the expansion of one's present existence "toward an indefinitely open future."[7] When we forego liberty in favour of the comfortable and the familiar, we render ourselves objects rather than human beings. When others block our liberty, they make us objects. If one is responsible for one's own objectification, it is a moral failing; if someone else is responsible, it is oppression. Both, she says, are absolute evils. For Beauvoir, then, a woman who consents to her own objectification is morally blameworthy, but so is anyone who seeks to objectify her. Since, on Beauvoir's account, men are always

---

7   Beauvoir, 16.

seeking to render woman as Other, and as object, it is the feminine condition constantly to struggle against objectification.

Beauvoir's existentialist ethics

Beauvoir's disquisition against happiness is an expression of her existentialism, and in particular her existentialist ethics. What is existentialism exactly? In a nutshell, it is the philosophical position that existence precedes essence. Put differently, existentialists maintain that we are not born certain kinds of people; rather, we make ourselves the kinds of people that we are over a lifetime through our experiences. Moreover, they argue that we have a responsibility to make ourselves the best kinds of people we can. Thus, we must constantly challenge ourselves because only in so doing will we make ourselves the best we can, and to do anything less wastes the opportunity to make a person that is available to every human being.

Men or the patriarchy?

While Beauvoir is explicit that it is men who Other women, some more recent feminist scholars take a more systemic approach. Perhaps most notably, Black feminist scholar bell hooks argues that it is patriarchy as a system, not individual men, that relegates women to subordinate roles. Moreover, she argues that both men and women are disadvantaged by patriarchy. Under patriarchy, according to hooks, women are dominated, but men are forced into the role of dominators, a role that limits their access to full emotional well-being. "Patriarchy," writes hooks, "is the single most life-threatening disease affecting the male body and spirit in our nation."[8] To put this in Beauvoir's terms, for hooks, the roles of both One and Other are imposed on, respectively, men and women, and both men and women suffer as a consequence.

---

8   bell hooks, "Understanding Patriarchy," 17. Note that she spells her name with all lower-case letters.

4.3. Freud: The girl as research subject

At the outset of his "Some Psychical Consequences of the Anatomical Distinction Between the Sexes" (1925), father of psychoanalysis Sigmund Freud admits that in his earlier works, he only focused on boys' psychological development, assuming that his conclusions could be extrapolated to girls. However, in this late work, Freud considers the possibility that psychosexual development proceeds differently in girls than in boys. The possibility is, to Freud, so important that he must publish about it before having empirically confirmed his theory. He is, at this point, an old man, and worries that if he dies before publishing his new hypothesis, it will too long await discovery by others.

In very broad strokes, Freud's *modus operandi* was to explain adult neuroses (and other mental illness) via abnormal childhood psychosexual development. In his paradigmatic account of male development, Freud holds that young boys naturally pass through an Oedipal stage in which they desire their mothers and regard their fathers as rivals, this stage coming to an end when sight of the female's (and hence the mother's) absence of a penis leads to the fear of castration and a withdrawal from the mother. According to Freud, normal male development thus includes a narcissistic interest in the phallus that helps to explain male masturbation.

Freud says that the main difference between normal male and female psychosexual development is that, unlike boys, girls replace their mothers with their fathers as the objects of affection. It is in the hopes of explaining this difference that Freud undertakes his inchoate research on female psychosexual development.

When a little girl sees a penis and hence realizes that she doesn't have one, Freud reports, she feels that her penis has been castrated. "She makes her judgement and her decision in a flash. She has seen it and knows that she is without it and wants to have it."[9] Once the girl realizes that all women lack a penis, Freud elaborates, she comes to regard females as inferior to males and begins to regard the lesser female sex with contempt. She blames her mother for her

---

9   Sigmund Freud, "Some Psychical Consequences of the Anatomical Distinction between the Sexes," 252.

own lack of a penis, and due to this alienation from the mother develops a particular tenderness toward her father. Some further consequences of female penis-envy Freud lists are a female tendency toward jealousy, a dislike of masturbation (since, on Freud's account, normal, well-adjusted girls do not wish to touch the site of their deficiency), and a range of feminine character traits, for instance, "that [women] show less sense of justice than men, that they are less ready to submit to the great exigencies of life, that they are more often influenced in their judgements by feelings of affection or hostility."[10] Freud cautions that "we must not allow ourselves to be deflected from such conclusions by the denials of the feminists, who are anxious to force us to regard the two sexes as completely equal in position and worth," but he admits that "the majority of men are also far behind the masculine ideal."[11]

While Freud was, in some respects, ahead of his time for considering female development separately from male (as he does in the text we are here discussing), it cannot escape one's attention that the model remains extremely male-centred. Just as in earlier works he uses the boy's discovery of a girl's lack of a penis to explain male psychosexual development, so in this late work he uses the girl's discovery of the boy's penis as an explanatory mechanism.

Although he was hugely influential in the history of psychology, Freud is no longer taken seriously by most academic psychologists and psychiatrists, but aspects of his approach remain influential (directly and indirectly) in both psychoanalytic and literary theory circles. Moreover, as we shall see in Chapters 7 and 8, Freud's view that human psychosexual identity forms during childhood was a key contributor to late twentieth-century clinical approaches to intersex infants and trans people. The great twentieth-century philosopher of science Karl Popper described Freudian psychoanalytic theory as "pseudoscience" because the theory adapted to accommodate any evidence and, hence, could not be falsified.

Notice, however, that neither of these explanatory mechanisms involves the discovery of the vulva. For Freud, the vagina is not a

---

10   Freud, 257–58.
11   Freud, 258.

distinct sexual organ, but rather the absence of a sexual organ. Thus, he does not allow for the possibility that a girl might be delighted to discover that she has a vulva but her brother doesn't; nor, does he conceive the possibility of a boy's experiencing vulva-envy. Despite Freud's express desire to consider girls on their own terms, he cannot help comparing them with boys, and doing so unfavourably. For Freud, the penis is the standard human genital. If—as in the case of females—one doesn't have it, then it constitutes a kind of lack. Thus, both physiologically and psychologically, the woman remains (in Beauvoir's terms) the Other, for Freud.

4.4. Irigaray: Écriture féminine

In her famous essay "This Sex Which Is Not One" (1985), feminist philosopher and psychoanalyst Luce Irigaray develops the method of "écriture féminine" (*feminine* or *women's writing*) first pioneered by her colleague, Hélène Cixous. Irigaray and Cixous argue that conventional forms of linguistic expression are, in fact, *masculine* forms of linguistic expression—that men and women naturally think and communicate differently from each other, and that feminine modes of communication have been effaced and elided. In their method of "écriture féminine," they seek to develop a distinctively feminine mode of communicating, one that derives naturally from female embodiment and psychology.

Irigaray's essay is steeped in the psychoanalytic tradition. Just as Freud held that having a penis affects one's view of the world and one's behaviour within it, so Irigaray argues that having a vagina causes one to think, feel and communicate differently. Where Freud traces the purported consequences of having or not having a penis, Irigaray considers the consequences of having or not having a vagina. It might even be helpful to think of Irigaray's text as a kind of parody of Freudian thought. However, it is not *only* a parody. Like Cixous before her, Irigaray genuinely seeks to develop and employ a new (or perhaps a very old) feminine language.

For Irigaray, at the heart of male and female difference is female sexual sufficiency compared to male sexual insufficiency. Whereas a male, to achieve sexual pleasure, needs something else—a vagina, an anus, a mouth, a hand, an inanimate object—to touch his penis, the female's two vaginal lips are always in contact. Thus, according to Irigaray, women experience constant low level sexual pleasure, whereas sexual pleasure for men is sporadic and bimodal (he is either experiencing heightened pleasure or experiencing no pleasure at all). Women, hence, have a kind of completeness born of the sense of touch. By contrast, men must use their eyes to find the things that will bring them pleasure. Irigaray argues that this key difference plays out into two very different ways of being in the world.

According to Irigaray, since the man requires some other thing—a tool, orifice, or appendage—to achieve sexual pleasure, he is always on the look-out for that thing. This has two psycho-cognitive consequences for him, she reports. First, he sees the world in terms of self and other (notice Beauvoir's influence here!), and second he privileges vision among all of his senses since vision more than any other sense brings distant others within range. Irigaray represents the male as forever sorting and categorizing the world in a binary way grounded in the self/other distinction.

By contrast, Irigaray characterizes woman as experiencing the world holistically precisely because she is already complete and does not require some other in order to achieve sexual satisfaction. Since woman's completeness derives from her two lips that are always touching, Irigaray thinks that it is the sense of touch, not sight, that is particularly central in female experience. Finally, and most crucially for the idea of écriture féminine, since woman need not sort the world into one and other, she does not understand the world according to a binary logic. This means that she does not, if she is being true to herself, think or speak in a way that seems logical within the context of male-dominated binaristic thinking. Irigaray writes:

> This is doubtless why she is said to be whimsical, incomprehensible, agitated, capricious ... not to mention her language, in which "she" sets off in all directions leaving "him" unable to discern the coherence of any meaning. Hers are contradictory words, somewhat mad from the standpoint of reason, inaudible for whoever listens to them with ready-made grids, with a fully elaborated code in hand. For in what she says, too, at least when she dares, woman is constantly touching herself.[12]

---

12   Luce Irigaray, "This Sex Which Is Not One," 28–29.

If women are sometimes thought to be less logical or articulate than men, Irigaray suggests, it is because they are being judged by a male standard of logic and language. (We'll encounter something very close to this idea in Chapter 11 when we consider Rousseau's advice for the education of girls.)

In treating the vagina as in many respects superior to the penis, and in considering men's lack of vaginas rather than women's lack of penises, Irigaray arguably inverts the usual One/Other opposition—situating woman as the One and man as the Other. However, even while promoting a female renunciation of heterosexuality, Irigaray cautions against lesbian separatism (roughly, the radical view that the best answer to patriarchy is to live as a lesbian and to focus one's efforts on lesbian communities. We'll look at this view again in Chapter 8). This variety of feminism, she thinks, risks containing women in "a new prison, a new cloister."[13] She argues that women must, for a time, remain separate from men in order to learn about the character of their own desire and about their own authentically feminine way of navigating in the world. However, she continues, if we aim "simply to reverse the order of things, even supposing this to be possible, history would repeat itself in the long run, would revert to sameness: to phallocratism—the ideology of 'penis-rule,' i.e., masculine power and dominance. It would leave room neither for women's sexuality, nor for women's imaginary, nor for women's language to take (their) place."[14] To view the world as One and Other, for Irigaray, is already, necessarily to view the world in a masculine way.

4.5. Questions for reflection

- According to Beauvoir, the fact that we are urged to remain women shows that "woman" is not a neutral species term but a term used to construct some people in certain ways. Might one make a similar argument about "man" and phrases such as "Be a man!"? What about other terms—terms related to ethnicity, (dis)ability, or sexual orientation, for instance?

---

13 Irigaray, 33.
14 Irigaray, 33.

- Unlike Beauvoir, who is primarily concerned with socio-cultural factors, both Freud and Irigaray strongly emphasize embodiment and sexuality. Which approach, in general, do you favour? Why? Does either approach exclude any groups? Members of religious or sexual minorities, for instance? If so, how? If not, why not?
- Is Beauvoir's existentialist ethics consistent with psychoanalytic approaches like Freud's and Irigaray's? Why or why not?

4.6. Works cited and recommended reading

Beauvoir, Simone de. *The Second Sex*. Trans. Constance Borde and Sheila Malovany-Chevallier. New York: Vintage, 2011.

Canadian Institutes of Health Research—Institute of Gender and Health. *What a Difference Sex and Gender Make: A Gender, Sex and Health Research Casebook*. <http://www.cihr-irsc.gc.ca/e/44734.html>. Accessed 27 April 2015.

Freud, Sigmund. "Some Psychical Consequences of the Anatomical Distinction between the Sexes." *The Standard Edition of the Complete Psychological Works of Sigmund Freud*. Vol. 19. Trans. James Strachey. London: Hogarth Press, 1961. 248–58.

Gulati, Martha and Henry R. Black. "Heart Rate Response to Exercise Stress Testing in Asymptomatic Women: The St. James Women Take Heart Project." *Circulation* 122.2 (2010): 130–37.

hooks, bell. "Understanding Patriarchy." *The Will to Change: Men, Masculinity, and Love*. New York: Atria, 2004. 17–34.

Irigaray, Luce. "This Sex Which Is Not One." *This Sex Which Is Not One*. Ithaca: Cornell University Press, 1985. 23–33.

Weissmann, Jordan. "Female Crash Dummies Part of Updated Vehicle Safety Tests." *The Washington Post*, 9 July 2008. <http://www.washingtonpost.com/wp-dyn/content/article/2008/07/08/AR2008070802661.html?hpid=sec-business&sslid=33252>. Accessed 27 April 2015.

CHAPTER 5

The Third Sex

5.1. More than two sexes?

The idea that there are only two sexes, and that they are in some sense opposite to each other is ubiquitous. It even occurs, by way of useful metaphor, in electronics and plumbing where plugs are often described as "male" and sockets described as "female." Is it inconceivable that there might be more than two sexes?

Despite the apparent inevitability of the two-sex model, some examples from biology show that two isn't necessarily a magic number when it comes to sex. Papaya trees come in three sexes—male, female, and hermaphroditic. So do some species of harvester ants, in which there are two separate types of phenotypically male ants—those who can only sire female workers and those who can sire reproductive females. Since both of these so-called mating types are necessary for the continued survival of the species, it is plausible to think of them as two distinct sexes (giving the species a total of three sexes). Some lichens and fungi have thousands of mating types.

There is no record of anyone ever seriously proposing that the human species has thousands of sexes. However, in ancient Athens and later in nineteenth-century Germany, it was suggested that it might have three. While the ancient account was not likely intended seriously, it has seized people's imaginations for centuries. Indeed, it was an influence on the German proposal, which was intended as a serious scientific hypothesis. Moreover, both accounts were influences on Freud, from whom we already heard in Chapter 4, and who will continue to make appearances in the remainder of this volume, so great was his influence on people's beliefs about human sexuality.

5.2. Plato's three sexes

The great Greek philosopher, Plato (427–347 BCE), communicated his philosophy through a series of dialogues that featured actual historical figures from ancient Athens. In many of these dialogues, his teacher, Socrates (470–399 BCE), appears as a character. In general, his remarks hew closely to Plato's own views. *Symposium* (c. 385–380 BCE) is one of the most beautiful and interesting of Plato's dialogues. As the dialogue opens, we learn that the Athenians gathered together for a banquet have been partying too hard of late. Thus, they decide that instead of more drinking and partying, they will devote the evening to debating the origin and nature of love. One after another, they take turns elaborating their accounts of love.

When his turn arrives, Aristophanes elaborates his myth of the three sexes. Once upon a time, he says, human beings were like big barrels with four arms, four legs, two faces, and so on. They were each essentially two modern people stuck together. There were then not two, but three sexes—the sun people were composites of two men; the earth people were composites of two women and the moon people were, as Aristophanes says, "hermaphrodites," composed as they were of both a man and a woman.

These four-legged people were so powerful that they became arrogant and impudent, and ceased to offer the gods their due. So, Zeus cut them in half. A sun person was divided into two men, an earth person into two women, and a moon person into a man and a woman. After this division, the halves were so devastated by the separation from their partners that they would not do anything other than cling to each other. They "died of starvation and general idleness because they would not do anything apart from each other.

When one of the halves died and the other was left, the half which was left hunted for another and embraced it ... and so they perished."[1]

Out of pity, Zeus created sexual reproduction so that the halved people could achieve some satisfaction and generation in their union, and thus get on with their lives. This, according to Aristophanes, was the origin of love.

Notice that Aristophanes's myth accounts for both heterosexual and homosexual desire. Sun men desire other men, while moon men desire women. Earth women desire other women, while moon women desire men. Indeed, in order to know which of the original three sexes a person belongs to, one would need to know about both their anatomy (Is it male or female?) and the nature of their desire (Are they attracted to males or females?).

As strange to us as it may seem, notice that an account of sex like Aristophanes's, which includes both an anatomical aspect and an aspect related to sexual activity, is actually quite similar to the harvester ant example we looked at above. With Aristophanic humans, just as with harvester ants, full knowledge of one's biological sex involves a couple of distinct components. One is not enough. There is, in fact, a good biological basis for taking a more complex view of sex than we usually do. In Chapter 7, we will return to that issue.

While some scholars occasionally attribute to Plato the account of the three sexes propounded here by Aristophanes, there is good reason to be cautious about this view. The real Aristophanes, a great satirical playwright, had ridiculed Plato's teacher, Socrates, in his play The Clouds (423 BCE). There, he represents Socrates as being so out of touch with reality that he hangs in the sky in a basket eating lettuce rather than standing on the ground with other men. It is quite plausible that, in Symposium, Plato sought to return the favour by putting what he regarded as a ridiculous view in Aristophanes's mouth. While Aristophanes was a real historical figure, there is no evidence that he himself held the view about love and the original three sexes that Plato attributes to him in the dialogue. Whatever the view's provenance, and whatever

1   Plato, *Symposium*, in *Great Dialogues of Plato*, 87.

Plato himself may have thought of the account, it is one that has for centuries captured people's imaginations. From Hermeticism (an esoteric movement that persisted from late antiquity to the renaissance) and nineteenth-century romanticism, to the early psychology and sexology of the nineteenth and twentieth centuries, the myth of the three sexes has for centuries been deployed and adapted in a variety of ways.

The surprising thing about Aristophanes's account (apart from the number of sexes he proposes) is that it is not heteronormative. That is, as opposed to those cultural artifacts that treat heterosexuality as the norm and other sexual identities as exceptions to be explained, Aristophanes's story treats homosexuality as just as normal as heterosexuality. Two of his three original sexes are homosexual, after all. More than this, though, Aristophanes problematizes the heterosexual sex as hermaphroditic, and goes on to diminish the people descended from the heterosexual pairing. "Adulterers generally come of that sex," he writes, "and all women who are mad for men, and adulteresses."[2] He has less to say about women who desire women, although he is clear that "strumpetesses"[3] number among them. Men who desire men, though, he discusses at length and in glowing terms. According to Aristophanes, such men are doubly manly in that they possess all of the manly virtues, and moreover desire others who do.

Aristophanes is not the only figure in *Symposium* who praises the love between two males. Earlier in the dialogue, Pausanias—the lifelong lover of Agathon, at whose home the banquet occurs—argues that men's love for women is "common" and merely physical, while men's love for other men is more noble, transcending the merely physical. Moreover, he argues, the love between an older man and a younger boy has an educative character, with the older man sharing with his beloved his own wisdom and experience.[4]

---

2   Plato, 87.
3   Plato, 87.
4   Plato, 78–79.

Even though the Aristophanic model seems on its face to pose an alternative to the view that there are two and only two sexes, it is worth noting that Aristophanes's three sexes are ultimately just combinations of male and female. His three-sex model is thus reducible to the familiar two-sex model. Moreover, even though Aristophanes's myth is accepting of homosexuality, it leaves no room for bisexuality (attraction to both males and females), asexuality (feeling no sexual desire), or pansexuality (attraction to people, irrespective of their gender). It also assumes as the norm lifelong monogamy, and implicitly rejects both serial monogamy and poly-amory (romantic relationships involving more than two partners). So, while it is in some senses quite "progressive," it is also conser-vative in many ways.

5.3. The Austro-German connection: Ulrichs, Hirschfeld, and Freud

While Plato did not intend the Aristophanic three sex model as scientific, Karl Heinrich Ulrichs (1825–95) saw in the Aristophanic model a possible basis for a science of sexual desire. Ulrichs, an early German sexologist and himself an out homosexual, sought a scientific explanation for homosexual desire. Inspired by the Aristophanic myth, he divided all human beings into three sexes: male dionians, female dionians, and uranians. By "dionian," Ulrichs meant any cisgender person who is attracted only to members of the opposite sex. He used "uranian" as an umbrella term for anyone who did not fit into either of the dionian categories. Thus, intersex and transgender people, homosexuals, bisexuals, and other sexual minorities are all, in Ulrichs's terminology, *uranian*.

"Intersex" refers to people born with ambiguous genitalia, with sex chromosome abnormalities, or with some misalignment between their sex chromosomes and their anatomy. We'll look more closely at intersex in Chapter 7.

"Transgender" is the term for someone whose gender identity does not align with their gender assignment at birth. We'll focus on transgender identities and issues in Chapter 8.

"Cisgender" is the term for someone who is not transgender. If you are cisgender, then your gender identity aligns with your gender assignment at birth. For example, you were born a female and you regard yourself as a female. The term is a fairly recent coinage, and one that Ulrichs did not have at his disposal.

Despite his own homosexuality, Ulrichs assumed that all sexual attraction is fundamentally attraction to the opposite sex. Thus, his main project was to understand how, despite this basic fact, uranians could have same-sex desires. He hypothesized that human beings have, lurking invisibly below their apparent biological sex, other, deeper sexual characters. Thus, someone externally male might have imperceptible female aspects, termed "germs," which are already present at the embryonic stage. To employ a familiar cliché (one that Ulrichs himself did not use), we might describe such a person as "a woman trapped in a man's body." That man's invisible female nature would entail that he is attracted to men, not women. Note that in Ulrich's terms, this still counts as attraction to the opposite sex, since it is not the outer man that desires other men in the case of homosexual desire. Rather, it is the inner female nature of the homosexual man that draws him to other men. Again, for Ulrichs, all sexual attraction is directed toward the opposite sex.

It is important to note that, for Ulrichs, the woman trapped in a man's body is in fact herself part of the man's body (as opposed to being a disembodied soul). These deeper sexual natures are, on his account, somatic—that is, physical, not psychological. Indeed, he came to believe that, beneath the skin, many of us combine a variety of sexual traits in complex ways. For this reason, his uranian category came to include a wide range of possible sexualities. I might be 100 per cent female on the outside, but only 80 per cent female on the inside, with the 20 per cent of me that is male expressing itself in various ways.

There are important similarities and differences between the Aristophanic model and Ulrichs's model. Most obviously, of course, both involve three sexes. However, the sexes themselves are different, with Aristophanes recognizing two original homosexual sexes (sun people and earth people) and one heterosexual one (the hermaphroditic moon people), whereas Ulrichs recognizes two heterosexual sexes (dionian males and dionian females) and one homosexual one (uranians). In both models, it is necessary to know about both a person's anatomy and their desire in order to discern to which sex they belong, and in both models sexual desire is innate and somatic. However, whereas the Aristophanic model considers both same-sex attraction and opposite-sex attraction possible in their own right, Ulrichs rejects same-sex attraction as inconceivable and explains it as a kind of deep-down opposite-sex attraction. Nonetheless, Ulrichs's model makes possible a range of sexual identities and desires, while the Aristophanic model can only cope with four types of sexual identities (men attracted to men, men attracted to women, women attracted to men, women attracted to women).

Arguably, Ulrichs's main claim to fame was in influencing the great German sexologist and gay rights activist, Magnus Hirschfeld (1868–1935). While Hirschfeld took considerable inspiration from Ulrichs, he did not accept his three-sex model. Instead, he posited a range of sexual identities and forms of desire. According to Hirschfeld, between what Ulrichs termed dionian males and dionian females, there lay a continuum with a plurality of intermediaries. (In some respects, Hirschfeld's work anticipated Alfred Kinsey's famous "Heterosexual-Homosexual Rating Scale." Indeed, some scholars argue that Hirschfeld's account went further than Kinsey's.)

The Kinsey Scale

The so-called Kinsey Scale (actually, the Heterosexual-Homosexual Rating Scale) was developed in 1948 by Alfred Kinsey, Wardell Pomeroy, and Clyde Martin as a means of expressing those researchers' view that there are a range of human sexual orientations between heterosexuality and homosexuality. The seven-point scale ranges from "exclusively heterosexual" at 0 to "exclusively homosexual" at 6. Still today, some people identify according to their "Kinsey numbers." Asked about their sexual orientation, such a person might describe themselves as a "Kinsey 4" or similar.

Despite the differences between Ulrichs's and Hirschfeld's accounts, Freud lumped them in together and dismissed both models. Nonetheless, he too drew upon the Aristophanic myth. Tellingly, though, he only discussed the male-female Aristophanic sex (the moon sex), which he linked with the romantic notion of lovers as two halves of one soul; he neglected the male-male (sun) and female-female (earth) pairings altogether.

Unlike Aristophanes and Ulrichs, Freud's own account of sexual desire was psychological rather than somatic, and developmental rather than nativist. That is, he regarded the character of a person's desire as something that developed over their childhood rather than being something with which we are born. Unlike Ulrichs, he did not assume that desire is always desire for the opposite sex. However, he regarded same-sex desire as the consequence of improper child-hood psychosexual development. As we shall see in Chapters 7 and 8, Freud's account of sexuality came to have enormous influence in the twentieth century. Nonetheless, by the end of that century, his account was on the wane and scholars and LGBTQ activists were taking seriously some views that closely resemble aspects of Hirschfeld's thought and, indeed, of the Aristophanic myth.

5.4. Questions for reflection

- Which is more liberating—regarding sexual orientation as something one is born with or as something that develops over time? Why?
- Each of the models we have examined in this chapter draws a link between sex as a *category* and sexual desire. Do you think it makes sense to connect these two concepts? Why or why not?
- How does Ulrichs's view compare with Freud's? How do each of them compare with the view Plato attributes to Aristophanes? As you compare the three models, consider the following questions: Is the model somatic or psychological? Pre-natal or developmental? Which kinds of sexual attraction are explained by this model? Which are rendered inexplicable? Which are taken as requiring no explanation? Which sexual orientation, if any, is regarded as "natural"? Which sexual orientation, if any, is regarded as "best?"

5.5. Works cited and recommended reading

Groneberg, Michael. "Myth and Science around Gender and Sexuality: Eros and the Three Sexes in Plato's *Symposium*." *Diogenes* 208 (2005): 39–49.

The Kinsey Institute. *Kinsey's Heterosexual-Homosexual Rating Scale*. <http://www.kinseyinstitute.org/research/ak-hhscale.html>. Accessed 28 April 2015.

Plato. *Symposium*, in *Great Dialogues of Plato*. Ed. Eric Warmington and Phillip Rouse. Trans. W.H.D. Rouse. New York: Mentor, 1956. 69–117.

CHAPTER 6

The Third Gender

6.1. Cultural variations in gender categories

In the last chapter, we looked at two theories—one fictitious and one intended as science—postulating the existence of three human sexes. In this chapter, we move from the discussion of sexes to the discussion of genders. In other words, instead of looking at the sexes directly (however many of these there may be), we will consider the social functions and roles that given cultures associate with the sexes. Specifically, we'll look at two cultures and one subculture, each of which in one way or another adopts the view that there are three human genders. That is, while they regard the human species as having only two sexes, they think that members of the species express their gender in three—not two—different ways.

6.2. Third gender traditions in First Nations cultures

We begin our consideration of cultures that recognize three genders in the Canadian North, where traditional Inuit culture seems to recognize three genders, for both culturo-religious and economic reasons.

Canadian anthropologist Bernard Saladin d'Anglure is an expert on Inuit culture, and in particular on gender issues and shamanism within that culture. In a 2005 study, d'Anglure argues that other anthropologists have, for various reasons, wrongly regarded the Inuit as recognizing only two genders. Among those anthropologists d'Anglure is criticizing, he names the great French anthropologist Michel Mauss, who held that Inuit society, like all societies, "oscillates between two poles, an individualist pole and a 'communist' pole," where this overarching duality marks "the totality of the social, economic and religious life of a people."[1]

For d'Anglure, by contrast, the male-female division is more fundamental than the individual-community division. D'Anglure proposes that anthropologists like Mauss failed to detect the complexities associated with gender in Inuit culture precisely because they did not properly understand that gender distinctions form the basic conceptual framework for society. By contrast, d'Anglure takes these complexities seriously, and he maintains that in Inuit culture, the male-female divide is itself mediated by a third gender—a gender that is expressed by transvestism within culture.

> D'Anglure regards the gender division as a fundamental organizing principle of society, more fundamental even than that between individual and community. See the Chapter 9 discussion of Shulamith Firestone for an elaboration of a very similar view.

D'Anglure argues that even anthropologists who have recognized the role of "religious transvestism" among the Inuit have nevertheless tended to neglect it, usually as a result of the broader theoretical frameworks they bring to bear on their research. On the one hand, Marxists, committed to evolutionary accounts of society, regarded Inuit transvestism as a mere remnant of an earlier matriarchal culture. On the other hand, Freudians' overemphasis on sexuality, and their commitment to the duality of male and female forms of sexual desire, hampered their attempts to understand the phenomenon.

---

1   Bernard Saladin d'Anglure, "The 'Third Gender' of the Inuit," 134.

A note on transvestism

In mainstream North American culture, "transvestism" is often associated with the practice of cross-dressing in order to experience sexual pleasure. This sense of the term is owing to its usage as a diagnosis by the American Psychiatric Association, which classes "transvestic disorder" as a paraphilia (basically, a condition characterized by unhealthy sexual desires). This is not the sense of the term employed by d'Anglure. For d'Anglure, "transvestism" simply means dressing in the clothing of the opposite gender, without any psychiatric or sexual connotations.

D'Anglure attributes to Marxist anthropologists the view that religious transvestism—that is, transvestism that plays a part in a religious tradition—is merely a remnant of ancient matriarchal cultures. It is worth noting that there is today considerable skepticism among anthropologists over whether there have ever been any genuine matriarchies.

The phenomenon d'Anglure seeks to explain, and which gives rise to his theory of an Inuit third gender, is the Inuit practice of raising some biological females to dress and act as boys, and some biological males to dress and act as girls. D'Anglure traces this practice both through interviews with Inuit people and, indirectly, through two striking legends.

D'Anglure's interviews provide evidence of two broad motivations for gender-swapping among the Inuit—one economic and one, as he says, "cosmological." With respect to the former, d'Anglure reports that in families with a gender imbalance among offspring (i.e., all girls or all boys), it is common for one child to be raised as a member of the opposite gender in order to perform the duties associated with that gender. Thus, for instance, in an all-girl family, one daughter might be raised as a son so that she can help with the hunt. Conversely, in an all-boy family, one son might be raised as a daughter so that he can help with food preparation and clothing manufacture.

The cosmological motivation is less pragmatic, and more deeply rooted in Inuit spirituality, especially the role of ancestors within that spirituality. Sometimes, writes d'Anglure, a deceased ancestor will appear in a dream to a child's parents-to-be. This is interpreted as a sign that the ancestor wishes to return and live again through the child. In this case, the parents name the child after the ancestor and the child, regardless of its biological sex, is raised according to that ancestor's gender.

D'Anglure recounts two myths that provide further evidence of an Inuit third gender. In the first, a "strange man" dresses as a woman and adopts female gender roles, even (thanks to supernatural intervention) giving birth. However, the strange man's child is a baby whale, who ultimately helps the man by luring other whales to shore to be hunted by the man's brothers. D'Anglure discerns both economic and the cosmological aspects in the tale of the strange man. On the one hand, the strange man is one of many brothers, and rather than hunting takes up the female-gendered task of sewing. He thus contributes to gender role balance in the family. However, he also insists that he can't hunt: "I can't! I can't! I am like a woman. How can I when I'm made like this?"[2] His gender role identification would suggest that his gender-swapping is not just economically practical, but is grounded in his deeper sense of self, one d'Anglure traces to a deceased ancestor.

In the second myth, Itijjuaq too is incapable of performing the gendered tasks associated with her sex. She "could neither scrape skins, nor cut them to shape for making into clothes, nor sew. Nor was she capable of having children."[3] However, with the assistance of her deceased grandparents, she develops magical powers, and in particular the power to heal. Thanks to these powers, she acquires a status in the community more in keeping with a great man than with a woman. She has two husbands who love her, and other women scrape the skins her husbands bring back from the hunt, make clothes for her family, and even give her children to adopt. Again, while this story has clear economic aspects, the role of deceased ancestors is clear.

It is important to note that d'Anglure did most of his field work decades ago, and that Inuit culture has undergone considerable change since then. While many Inuit are working to preserve

---

2   D'Anglure, 135–36.
3   D'Anglure, 139.

traditional language and culture, fewer and fewer Inuit enter-
tain the kind of traditional beliefs that d'Anglure describes in his
article, for instance "that a mistreated child can become a giant
thirsting for revenge, or that a polar bear can be changed into an
Arctic fox if a menstruating woman looks at it, and that a dwarf
can become the size of his opponent."[4]

A third aspect of Inuit gender-swapping is also evident in both
stories—namely, that practice's connection to shamanism. Both the
strange man and Itijjuaq have supernatural powers and communicate with supernatural beings. The strange man parlays with the
Maker of All, while Itijjuaq communicates with her dead grandparents. On d'Anglure's account, there is a higher incidence of
shamanism among Inuit raised as the opposite gender than among
the population overall. His explanation for this is at the heart of his
claim that the Inuit third gender serves a mediatory function. For the
Inuit, says d'Anglure, one who could straddle genders in this way
"was also capable of straddling all boundaries, between the world
of humans and that of animals, between the dead and the living."[5]

Non-binary indigeneity

We have focused here on d'Anglure's view that Inuit culture recognizes three genders. However, it is by no means the only indigenous
culture that does so. From the fa'afafine of Samoa to Navajo nádleehí,
a number of indigenous cultures worldwide resist gender binarism.

You may also have heard the word "berdache." French settlers in the seventeenth and eighteenth centuries used this term
to describe North American First Nations people whose gender
expressions and gender roles did not align with their gender assignment at birth. In recent years, however, many First Nations people
and their allies have chosen to replace the term "berdache" with
the umbrella term "two spirit." Whereas "berdache" is a Eurasian
term that was imposed on First Nations people by settlers, "two
spirit" was coined by First Nations people themselves in order to

---

4   D'Anglure, 143.
5   D'Anglure, 138.

situate an array of non-cisgender identities within the framework of First Nations culture. While there are clear similarities between two spirit people and trans people, many people who identify as two spirit do not identify as trans. In some longer variants of the LGBTQ umbrella (for instance, LGBTTIQQ2S), a "2" is included to signify two spirit people.[6]

6.3. Hijras: Neither man nor woman?

In the popular press these days, the phrase "third gender" occurs most frequently in connection with hijras, third gender people found on the Indian subcontinent, in India, Pakistan, Bangladesh, and Nepal. The reason that hijras have been making the news is that, in recent years, all four of these countries have created a third gender status for hijras' legal documents, such as passports.

Serena Nanda's "The Hijras of India" provides us with a rare glimpse of hijra culture. It is a rare glimpse because, despite the fact that hijras are increasingly organizing themselves into solidarity groups and effectively lobbying for improved conditions, they still often resist talking to researchers or members of the media.

In Nanda's account of India's hijras, we can once again see both religious and economic explanations for the existence of a third gender. On the one hand, hijras constitute a religious community of ascetics devoted to the worship of the mother goddess Bahuchara Mata. In this capacity, they perform a ritual role at weddings and births. However, this role is itself part of the economic story, as many hijras come from extremely impoverished backgrounds, and adopting the hijra gender admits people into a supportive community in which it is possible to earn an income via such ritual roles

---

6   "LGBTTIQQ2S" stands for "lesbian, gay, bisexual, transsexual, transgender, intersex, queer, questioning, Two Spirit." This is one of several long acronyms devised with the hope of including all queer identities under a single rubric. These acronyms are so difficult to say and to remember, that some members of the queer community have instead begun using "QUILTBAG" ("Queer/Questioning, Intersex, Lesbian, Transgender/Two Spirit, Bisexual, Asexual/Ally, Gay/Genderqueer"). For convenience and because it is more familiar to non-LGBTQ readers, I use "LGBTQ" throughout this volume.

and, for some, via paid sex work. Nanda notes, however, that these two forms of income stand in some tension. In the context of their religious role, hijras are supposed to be asexual (and, indeed, claim to abjure sexual relations); however, sex work is a main source of income for many of them.

Some cautions re: methodology, language, and culture

While Nanda's account of hijras is careful and scholarly, some caution is in order. Nanda is explicit about the methodological challenges inherent in her study of hijras. Hijras are extremely cautious with those outside their community. It is thus extremely difficult to get hijras to speak about themselves; indeed, few non-hijras in India ever have conversations with hijras.

Moreover, Nanda very often confesses her own inability to fully express aspects of hijra culture. She several times says that she lacks the vocabulary to express some concept. Indeed, notions of gender are so heavily embedded in particular cultures that translation of gender terms between two languages is often more problematic than other kinds of translation (already, a fraught business, as any second-language speaker knows). Don't be too quick to label hijras, or aspects of their culture, with North American terms. It may seem convenient to do so, but you risk effacing important differences between the two cultures.

Finally, at the opposite end of the continuum from effacing difference, there is the additional risk of exoticizing unfamiliar cultures—exaggerating what is strange, shocking, or puzzling about those cultures and thereby missing out on a more careful, nuanced understanding of them.

It is well to keep all of these cautions in mind when thinking about all of the cultures we are considering in this chapter.

In addition to religious and economic mechanisms, Nanda suggests two other factors that shape hijra identity: the factors of (a) gender identity (or gender-role identity), and (b) sexual orientation. Although, in strictness, hijras are regarded as neither male nor female, some of Nanda's interview subjects cite the desire to occupy female gender roles as among their reasons for becoming hijras. Others report having become hijras to escape ridicule by their communities for being too "feminine." While Nanda does not discuss the possibility that hijras are transgender (see Chapter 8 for a discussion of trans issues), this may be a plausible way to think about hijra identity. Remember though that gender identities are often constructed and described very differently in North American and Asian cultures; it might not even occur to Nanda's interviewees to describe themselves as transgender—that is, as having been assigned at birth with a gender not one's own.

Finally, with respect to sexual orientation, Nanda suggests that some men become hijras because they wish to have romantic/sexual relationships with men. Moreover, some of Nanda's interviewees related having been "spoiled" for sex with women due to early homosexual experiences. It is well to bear in mind, of course, that sexual orientation isn't just about having sex. Some hijras express a desire for romantic love with a man, quite apart from their sexual desire. Indeed, one of the appeals for men of a relationship with a hijra is that romantic love is de-emphasized in traditional arranged marriages, whereas a relationship with a hijra might be centrally motivated by romantic love.

Whatever the motivations for becoming hijra, it is clear that hijras are extremely vulnerable. They are socially ostracized, and even at the community events where they perform their religious rituals, they are regarded as embarrassing annoyances. They typically come from very poor backgrounds, and their low social status as hijras ensures that they remain poor, with few means of generating income available to them. They are shunned and abused, experiencing a high rate of violence. While they are beginning to make legal gains, many rights continue to elude them. Unlike members of the Inuit third gender, who are valued for their mediatory role, hijras are taboo.

6.4. "Aggressives": Third gender in the city

It is easy to imagine that cultures that embrace a third gender are all rural or distant. Daniel Peddle's 2005 documentary, *The Aggressives*, up-ends that view. Set in inner-city New York, the film explores the so-called aggressive or AG subculture—a predominantly African

American subculture of lesbians who identify as women but who adopt male gender roles, deriving their identity as *aggressives* from their performance of a stereotypical version of Black masculinity.

The film offers portraits of six self-identified aggressives. Ranging in age from the teens to their twenties, the six women have in common not only their distinctive gender role identity, but also an urban context characterized by poverty, racialization, and homophobia. For several of the film's subjects, their aggressive identity began in their attempt to reconcile their sexual orientation with the prevailing mores of their subculture. In one way or another, performing Black masculinity helps each of them to carve out a space for their lesbianism.

However, the aggressives are all explicit that their aggressive identity is not exhausted by their sexual orientation. All of them embrace the aesthetics of the masculine roles they adopt, as well as the power that masculinity affords them. Some of the aggressives sexually objectify women in various ways, while others elaborate on the masculine power they insist upon in sexual and romantic relationships: "I wear the pants," says an aggressive named Kisha.[7] In one striking scene set at a gay ball attended by aggressives, we see the most violent aspects of masculine power pantomimed in a song and dance routine with such overtly and shockingly misogynistic lyrics as "beat that bitch with a baseball bat."[8]

Gay balls are central to the social lives of the women portrayed in the film. These balls are parties, usually in nightclubs, at which members of the LGBTQ community gather for music, dancing, and drag contests. While some of the contestants in these contests project the kind of "camp" aesthetic that one often associates with popular representations of drag queens, the aggressives' drag performances lack the playfulness of camp. With seriousness and intensity, the aggressives perform such roles as "Wall Street" and construction worker. The only difference between their performance of Black masculinity at the balls and their usual performance of gender is often a prop, like a hard hat or a briefcase. The film portrays the aggressives as binding their breasts with duct tape, shaving their

---

7   Daniel Peddle, dir. *The Aggressives*.
8   *The Aggressives*.

heads, donning dental grills (decorative jewellery worn over the teeth), and being measured for suits not only in preparation for balls but as part of their day-to-day lives.

Gender as performative?

I described aggressives as performing Black masculinity. In what sense does one perform gender? Drag competitions show that one can perform gender just as one can perform a dramatic role. For instance, when a cis man portrays Marilyn Monroe in a drag competition, there can be no question that it is a performance. However, some gender theorists see the performance of gender as much more ubiquitous, and much more insidious, than this. Most notably, Judith Butler follows Kessler and McKenna (Remember these three scholars from Chapter 2?) in conceiving gender not as something that we *are* but as something that we *do*. While Kessler and McKenna focus on the way that we do gender when we perform a gender attribution, Butler emphasizes the way that we do gender by performing our gender identities. For Butler, gender is a highly regulated, culturally-significant repetition of acts. These acts include such mundane things as wearing a skirt or taking up less space on a subway seat. Importantly, she contrasts performing gender with expressing it. For Butler, we do not "have" underlying genders that we express in one way or another. Gender is nothing more than our performance of it. Put differently, gender is constituted by performance. For most of us most of the time, the various ways in which we perform our genders feel very natural, unconscious even. However, on Butler's account they feel this way because we repeat them over and over, not because they express our underlying nature. The core aim of Butler's project is to reveal the system of power that produces the performative repetition of gender.

If we compare aggressives to hijras and to third gender Inuit people, we can see more obvious similarities with hijras than with third gender Inuit. As with hijra identity, aggressive identity is strongly correlated to low socio-economic status, and to a marginalized sexual orientation. Moreover, aggressives enjoy solidarity and sociality with each other, just as hijras do. However, aggressive culture seems to lack the cosmological-spiritual aspect present in both hijra and Inuit third-gender culture.

What is striking about all three candidates for third-gender status we have considered in this chapter is the way in which the gender identities and gender roles in question seem to be composed of aspects of masculinity and femininity rather than transcending those categories. That masculinity and femininity can be combined in various ways suggests that they are not, as Aristotle thought, contrarieties.

Indeed, this was precisely the view of Sandra Bem (1944–2014), the pioneering American psychologist who famously challenged the idea that gender roles are mutually incompatible opposites.[9] Bem developed an instrument, the Bem Sex-Role Inventory (BSRI), to measure individuals' levels of masculinity, femininity, and androgyny. On Bem's account, while many people are highly masculine and not highly feminine, or highly feminine and not highly masculine, a person might be both highly masculine and highly feminine—she terms this combination "androgyny." (Singer Marilyn Manson or Johnny Depp's character Jack Sparrow might be examples of androgynous people.) Conversely, they might be low on both masculinity and femininity. Bem calls these people "undifferentiated." (Actor Tilda Swinton or rapper Angel Haze might fall into this category.)

While Bem intended the BSRI to be used on individuals, not cultures, it might be helpful to think about the cultural conceptualizations of gender—and of a third gender—we have been considering in this chapter against the framework of Bem's tool. What do you think? Would you characterize any of the gender expressions and gender identities we have surveyed in this chapter as masculine, feminine, androgynous, or undifferentiated? Does it help to think about cultural expressions of gender in this way? Does it help us to get clear on whether they are indeed instances of third genders? Does the notion of a third gender even make sense against a background that conceptualizes gender in terms of two opposite poles (as Chapter 5's Magnus Hirschfeld conceived of gender) or two orthogonal axes (as Bem conceived of it)? Is *two* somehow a magic number when it comes to gender?

---

9   Sandra Bem, "The Measurement of Psychological Androgyny," 155–62.

6.5. Questions for reflection

- Do you think any of the gender identities we've discussed in this chapter truly transcend the usual gender dichotomy? Why or why not?
- How do economic and "cultural" reasons for the third gender interact in Inuit culture? In Indian culture? How much do economic and cultural factors interact in your own lived experience of gender?
- Nanda discusses the inadequacy of English to capture aspects of hijra culture. How much of your own concept of gender is dictated by the language(s) you speak? If you speak more than one language, reflect on whether both or all of the languages you speak deal with gender and sexuality in the same way. If they're different, how are they different?
- In what ways do race and gender norms intersect in the case of aggressives? In what ways do they intersect in your own life? In the lives of those you know?

6.6. Works cited and recommended reading

Bem, Sandra. "The Measurement of Psychological Androgyny." *Journal of Clinical and Consulting Psychology* 42 (1974): 155–62.

D'Anglure, Bernard Saladin. "The 'Third Gender' of the Inuit." *Diogenes* 208 (2005): 134–44.

Nanda, Serena. "The Hijras of India." *A Queer World*. Ed. Martin Duberman. New York: New York University Press, 1997. 82–86.

Peddle, Daniel, dir. *The Aggressives*. Seventh Art Releasing, 2005.

Roscoe, Will. *Changing Ones: Third and Fourth Genders in Native North America*. New York: St. Martin's Press, 1998.

CHAPTER 7

Intersex

7.1. Dimorphism and deviation

In Chapter 5, we examined two models—Plato's and Ulrichs's—of human beings as divided into three rather than two sexes. In 1993, Brown University biologist Anne Fausto-Sterling provocatively suggested that there are actually five sexes. She based this argument on the incidence within human populations of what she termed "hermaphrodites"—roughly, human beings who display both male and female traits. Fausto-Sterling argued that human sex categories should include not only male and female, but also male pseudohermaphrodite, female pseudohermaphrodite, and true hermaphrodite.

How could sex be so complicated? Well, the kinds of features that we count as markers of biological sex include both genotype (genes and, in particular, chromosomes) and phenotype (an organism's observable physical characteristics). Phenotype gets further broken down into such things as appearance and function of both the internal and external sex organs, secondary sex traits such as breasts and beards, and production of and response to sex hormones. It turns out that, in all of these categories, human beings occur in more than two varieties.

Deviation from typical human sexual dimorphism occurs in three broad classes:

1. One or more reproductive organs are ambiguous or unusual as a result of underlying mechanisms involving sex chromosomes or sex hormone production or reception (e.g., CAH—congenital adrenal hyperplasia).

2. Reproductive organs are ambiguous or unusual but who have no underlying sex chromosome or hormone irregularities (e.g., vaginal agenesis).

3. Sex chromosomes or hormones are irregular, but reproductive organs are not particularly ambiguous or unusual (e.g., Turner's syndrome).

While, inevitably, some critics attacked Fausto-Sterling for denying human sexual dimorphism, some scholars in the field charged Fausto-Sterling with oversimplifying the real complexity of human sexual biology. They argued that, in fact, there are so many different kinds of outliers from the categories of male and female that even five sexes aren't enough to capture them all.

What types of intersex conditions are there?

There is a wide range of intersex conditions, some but not all of which present as ambiguous genitalia. Blackless et al. (2000) is a great place to start to learn about these conditions. You might also want to check out the website of the now-disbanded Intersex Society of North America. The archived version of the ISNA's website remains an excellent source for information about intersex as a medical condition, but also about intersex identity and the history of intersex activism. It is important to remember that although all intersex conditions are biological in character, they do not all necessarily require medical intervention. Thus, the term "condition" may itself be inapt when describing intersex variation.

7.1.1. Hermaphrodite or intersex?

Before we go any further, it's worth saying a few words about "hermaphrodite" as a term. While the term was in use until late into the twentieth century, it is no longer used by scholars, clinicians, or activists to describe human beings who do not neatly fit into the category of male or female. Instead, such people are now generally termed "intersex." One reason for this is that the word "hermaphrodite," derived from Greek mythology (from Hermaphroditos, the son of Hermes and Aphrodite), risks representing people so categorized as somehow mystical or exotic. Intersex scholar and activist Morgan Holmes, for instance, worries that when people use "hermaphrodite," the term's mythological connotations contribute to a conception of intersex people as "extrahuman or subhuman."[1]

However, just as importantly, "hermaphroditism" remains a technical term in biology used in describing characteristics of entire species, and this too makes the term an awkward choice for describing specific human beings. Among the species that reproduce sexually, there are two broad types: gonochoristic and hermaphroditic. Members of gonochoristic species are normally either male or female, but not both, for their entire lifespan. This is not the case with hermaphroditic species, in which members normally possess both male and female organs, either at a time (simultaneous hermaphrodites) or over the course of their lifespan (sequential hermaphrodites). While most birds and mammals are gonochorists, many fish, amphibians, and plants are hermaphrodites of one sort or another. The important distinction between intersex people and hermaphrodites (in this sense of the term) is that the former deviate from a gonochoristic species norm while the latter are typical members of their species.

Simultaneous versus sequential hermaphrodites

Pseudobiceros flatworms are simultaneous hermaphrodites. All members produce both sperm and eggs. Each flatworm has two penises, but no vagina. They mate by rearing up and "fencing" with

---

1   Morgan Holmes, *Intersex: A Perilous Difference*, 163, n. 17.

their penises. The winner of the battle uses its penises to impale the loser and inserts sperm in the resulting wound. Most other species of simultaneous hermaphrodites reproduce less violently than pseudobiceros. The familiar earthworm, for example, has two pores that release sperm and two receptacles for receiving sperm. During intercourse, both earthworms use both their male and female sex organs, and both worms' eggs can be fertilized. For them, there is no winner or loser, no impaling and no scarring.

Clownfish (the fish featured in *Finding Nemo*) are sequential hermaphrodites. They are all born male. They live in colonies that include one female, one mating male, and a whole bunch of juvenile males. When the female dies, the mating male proceeds to its next developmental stage to become the new female, whereupon one of the juvenile males proceeds to its next developmental stage to become the new mating male. (Understanding this fact about clownfish turns *Finding Nemo* into a very different film—less a father-son bonding film than a romance! What do you think? Were the Disney writers who created the iconic children's film ignorant about clownfish biology or were they surprisingly subversive?)

7.1.2. The continuum view

Seven years after her controversial 1993 article, Fausto-Sterling was a co-author of an influential study (hereafter, Blackless et al.) that surveyed the incidence of various intersex conditions among North American live births. The study contrasts the real incidence of biological sex variation among humans with absolute dimorphism, which, it says, biologists and medical scientists recognize as "a Platonic ideal not actually achieved in the natural world."[2]

Platonic ideal?

What exactly do Blackless et al. mean when they refer to Platonic ideals? Plato believed that all finite things in existence were exemplars of ideals of their type. For Plato, the thing that connects two

2   Melanie Blackless et al., "How Sexually Dimorphic Are We? Review and Synthesis," 151.

horses such that we think of them both *as horses* is each horse's partaking of, and resemblance to, a fixed essence possessed by all horses. For Plato this essence or *ideal* is perfect, unchanging and eternal. Thus, when Blackless et al. refer to absolute dimorphism as a Platonic ideal, they mean that it is unattainable by finite things.

According to Blackless et al., however, these same biologists and scientists in general nonetheless believe that there is a "correct developmental pathway" for each sex, even though most individuals approximate to this pathway imperfectly. Blackless et al. recommend in place of "absolute dimorphism" a characterization of human sexual variation as occurring on a "bimodal continuum," with "complete maleness" and "complete femaleness" located at either end:

Complete maleness and complete femaleness represent the extreme ends of a spectrum of possible body types. That these extreme ends are the most frequent has lent credence to the idea that they are not only natural (that is, produced by nature) but normal (that is, they represent both a statistical and social ideal). Knowledge of biological variation, however, allows us to conceptualize the less frequent middle spaces as natural, although statistically unusual.[3]

While the continuum model has considerable appeal, it is not uncontroversial. In 2002, the sometime physician, psychologist, and founder of the National Association for Single Sex Public Education, Leonard Sax, published a stinging reply to Blackless et al.'s continuum approach, in which he argued that "human sexuality is a dichotomy, not a continuum."[4]

The disagreement between continuum proponents and absolute dimorphism proponents primarily hinges not on the data surrounding human sexual variation, but on terminology. (Indeed, Sax uses Blackless et al.'s data in his article.) Blackless et al. use the term "intersex" to refer to any "individual who deviates from the Platonic ideal of physical dimorphism at the chromosomal, genital, gonadal,

3   Blackless et al., 76.
4   L. Sax, "How Common Is Intersex? A Response to Anne Fausto-Sterling," 177.

or hormonal levels."[5] Defined this way, intersex has an incidence of about 1.7 per cent. Against this usage, Sax argues that "deviation from the Platonic ideal" is not a clinically useful definition, and that "a definition of intersex which encompasses individuals who are phenotypically indistinguishable from normal is likely to confuse both clinicians and patients."[6] Sax offers as a "comprehensive, yet still clinically useful definition of intersex ... those conditions in which (a) the phenotype is not classifiable as either male or female, or (b) chromosomal sex is inconsistent with phenotypic sex."[7] Adopting this definition for "intersex" would exclude by far the commonest of the conditions included in Blackless et al.'s definition, late-onset congenital adrenal hyperplasia (LOCAH), as well as sex chromosome aneuploidies (conditions characterized by an unusual number of chromosomes in a cell, such as Turner's syndrome and Klinefelter syndrome), and vaginal agenesis. Excluding these conditions means excluding about 99 per cent of the cases Blackless et al. document. Based on Sax's definition, intersex individuals comprise only two out of every 10 000 live births, or about .02 percent of the population. That is, if we accept Sax's definition of "intersex," then the incidence of intersex births is only about 1/100th of the 1.7 per cent that Blackless et al. claim.

Despite the two opposing sides' efforts to nail down the frequency of intersex births, it is arguable that the numbers don't make any real difference to either of them. All that the continuum proponents need to represent sex as a bimodal continuum is two bell curves with overlapping tails, as in figure 7.1. Taking one curve to represent the male typicality, and the other to represent female typicality, we can think of the shaded area where the two curves overlap as representing the incidence of intersex. Following Sax's definition of "intersex" would mean that the area of overlap is smaller than it would be according to the definition given by Blackless et al., but both accounts will acknowledge that there is such an area, so both accounts seem committed to some degree of continuity.

---

5   Blackless et al., 161.
6   Sax, 175.
7   Sax, 2.

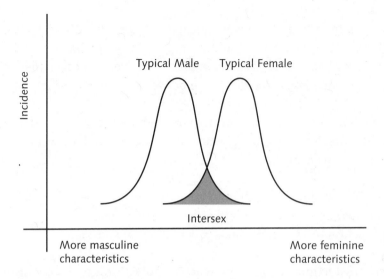

Figure 7.1: Sex as a bimodal continuum, from Melanie Blackless, Anthony Charuvastra, Amanda Derryck, Anne Fausto-Sterling, Karl Lauzanne, and Ellen Lee, "How Sexually Dimorphic Are We? Review and Synthesis," *American Journal of Human Biology* 12 (2000): 151–66

Arguably, it doesn't really matter whether .02 per cent or 1.7 per cent of the population are situated on those overlapping tails. For Sax's part, what's important is not the incidence of intersex, but its pathological nature. From a clinical perspective, a category such as "intersex" is deployed as part of the process of diagnosis and treatment. If a condition requires neither diagnosis nor treatment, then there is no need to include it under the rubric of a clinical term.

There are many other instances, besides intersex, of people who con-siderably deviate from human species norms in one or more respects. Consider the Olympic swimmer, Michael Phelps. His lung capacity and arm-length to torso-length ratio are both way higher than the norm for human beings. We don't pathologize such traits, however, probably because they contribute to his astonishing prowess as a swimmer. It seems to reveal a puzzling double standard, then, that considerable stigma was attached to the discovery that South African elite runner Caster Semenya is chromosomally male, despite her female external organs. Some critics argued that Semenya's intersex condition gave her an unfair advantage over other female athletes. However, it is well known that Phelps's lung capacity and long arms give him a considerable advantage over other swimmers. What, if anything, is the difference between these two cases?

Indeed, the crucial point at issue between the two sides is whether intersex is normal or natural. Blackless et al.'s continuum inference runs as follows:

Premise 1: Intersex conditions are naturally occurring.
Premise 2: Anything naturally occurring is normal.
Conclusion: Therefore, intersex conditions are normal.

By contrast, clinicians like Sax who support absolute dimorphism argue as follows:

Premise 1: Intersex conditions require clinical intervention.
Premise 2: Nothing requiring clinical intervention is normal.
Conclusion: Intersex conditions are not normal.

While the latter approach is clearly of greater clinical utility than the former, we need to be extremely cautious about definitions of "intersex" that take the need for clinical intervention as their starting point. Since the clinical conception of intersex is treatment-oriented, it follows *ex hypothesi* that intersex people require treatment.

However, whether or not such treatment is actually required is one of the points at issue. While some intersex conditions are associated with health risks requiring medical treatment (salt-wasting in people with CAH, for instance), many of the medical interventions on intersex people are solely aesthetic, performed with the goal of normalizing the patient.

Indeed, bioethicist and medical historian Alice Dreger argues that twentieth-century advances in surgery, and with them increasing mechanisms for normalizing intersex patients, actually drove a large shift in the medical understanding of intersex. Prior to the twentieth century, Dreger reports, clinicians faced with determining the "true sex" of intersex people sought answers in patients' gonadal tissue. In the period Dreger dubs the "age of gonads,"[8] an intersex person, no matter their morphology and gender identity, was judged female if they had ovarian tissue and male if they had testicular tissue. In those very rare cases in which both ovarian and testicular tissue were present in the gonads, the patient was dubbed a "true hermaphrodite."

Dreger surveys evidence that using gonadal tissue as the arbiter of sex developed as a means of reinforcing the ideology that everyone has one and only one true sex that awaits discovery, and that there are only two distinct sexes. However, the tension between patients' morphology, gender identity, and gender roles, on the one hand, and their gonadal tissue, on the other hand, threatened to break down the so-called "one-body-one-sex"[9] rule. With the discovery of sex chromosomes at the end of the nineteenth century, gonadal tissue had new competition for its role as arbiter of "true sex." Moreover, with the development of new surgical and hormonal technologies came new methods of normalizing intersex patients in order to avoid obvious misalignment among their various sex traits—misalignments that threatened to raise doubts about the ideology of sexual binarism. Thus, argues Dreger, rather than discovering patients' "true sex" through gonadal examination, the medical establishment arrived at a newer, more powerful means of reinforcing the "one-body-one-sex rule" by surgically and hormonally reconstructing intersex patients as uncontroversially male or female. Put differently, Dreger takes the radical view that surgical and hormonal interventions with intersex patients were (and are!) chiefly intended to reinforce the ideology of sexual binarism, and only secondarily intended to improve those patients' well-being.

Whether clinical approaches to intersex are primarily motivated by ideology or by concern for patients, there is mounting evidence that intersex people suffer more from the pathologization of their condition and the consequent medical interventions to "correct" their condition than they do from their ambiguous genitalia, etc. Considerable anecdotal evidence is emerging concerning the adverse

8   Alice Dreger, *Hermaphrodites and the Medical Invention of Sex*, 139.
9   Dreger, 30.

pyscho-social effects of pediatric gender reassignment. Moreover, the long-term failure rates for genital sensation among patients who have received pediatric gender reassignment surgery are between 20 per cent and 30 per cent. By contrast, some intersex conditions, like clitoromegaly—enlarged clitoris—left untreated, may actually increase rather than diminish the possibilities for giving and receiving sexual pleasure. Put simply, the medicalization of intersex conditions can lead to both psychological and sexual suffering.

7.2. Intersex infants and medical ethics

Suzanne Kessler (remember her from Chapter 2?) sheds some light on this question in a 1990 report on interviews she did with six New York area pediatric intersex specialists. Kessler argues that cultural factors often outweigh biological ones in clinicians' judgments about and treatment of ambiguously sexed infants but that the clinicians themselves are not adequately aware of the weight of these cultural factors. While medical science now permits the ready identification of a child's chromosomal and hormonal sex, Kessler's study shows that clinicians often privilege cultural and aesthetic factors such as penis length over sex chromosomes. Moreover, on Kessler's account, despite biological exceptions to sexual dimorphism, medical practitioners are antecedently committed to the view that a person must belong to one sex or another, but not both—a bias that affects their clinical judgments.

The developmental account of gender identity

Kessler attributes developmental theories of gender identity in Psychology with largely influencing clinicians' approaches to intersex infants. A developmental account holds that gender identity develops over time, in ways that are affected by various psychosocial factors, rather than being "built-in" at birth. The debate over whether gender identity is developmental or innate parallels a similar debate with regard to sexual orientation. Within the context of sexual orientation, LGBTQ people, including activists and scholars, very often incline toward the view that sexual orientation is innate. Hence, the slogan recently popularized by Lady Gaga, "Born this way." By contrast, conservatives outside of the LGBTQ community are often sympathetic to the developmental argument. This helps to explain why some of those conservatives believe that so-called conversion therapy may be an effective "cure" for homosexuality.

The developmental account, as applied to both gender identity and sexual orientation, has its roots in Freudian psychoanalysis. Recall from Chapter 5 that Freud regarded gender as psychological and developmental rather than somatic and innate. The route from Freud to 1980s and 1990s era urologists goes by way of early trans people and their psychologists. The first genital reconstruction surgeries were performed on trans people. Since transgenderism was considered a variety of mental illness, trans people underwent psychiatric assessment and care before undergoing sex reassignment surgery. (We'll look more closely at that topic in Chapter 8.) Thus, the first genital reconstruction surgeries occurred in a context dominated by psychologists, still in those days very much under the sway of Freudian theory. This same theory was lightly modified and applied to intersex people.

The main figure behind this movement was American psychologist, John Money. Kessler notes that when she conducted her interviews, treatment protocols for intersex patients were directly and indirectly dominated by Money's theories. They were for a time "the only game in town" when it came to intersex.

In Canada, Money is perhaps best remembered as the controversial psychologist at the centre of the David Reimer sex change controversy. Reimer, a Canadian, was born Bruce. After a botched circumcision irrevocably damaged his penis, Money counselled performing sex reassignment surgery and raising Bruce as a girl—Brenda. For years, Money cited this case as evidence of the fluidity of gender identity, and hence as providing evidential support for developmental theories of gender identity. However, during puberty, Reimer ceased to identify as a girl, and eventually transitioned back to male. Reimer's lifelong depression and ultimate suicide are regarded by many as the consequence of the gender (re)construction Money had advised.

Kessler identifies three main factors as together forming the foundation of attitudes toward intersex at the time of her research:

1. Advancements in surgical techniques and endocrinology make the surgical (re)construction of genitalia possible.
2. Thanks to feminism, reproduction is no longer considered women's primary function. Thus, the type of gonadal tissue in a patient is considered less crucial in determining sex than previously.
3. Developmental psychologists' emphasis on gender identity led to the belief that gender identity is fluid and distinct from biological sex, making it possible to successfully cultivate either male or female gender identity in a child so long as the process begins early enough.

According to Kessler's interviewees, the main source for their treatment of intersex patients is Money and Ehrhardt's classic 1972 volume, *Man & Woman, Boy & Girl*.[10] Money and Ehrhardt maintained—and Kessler's interviewees believed—that gender identity is changeable until about 18 months. An intersex infant can be successfully "constructed" as either male or female regardless of chromosomal gender provided that:

1. The parents have no doubt about the child's sex.
2. The genitals are reconstructed to match the assigned gender as soon as possible.
3. Gender-appropriate hormones are administered at puberty.
4. The patient is kept aware of their condition with age-appropriate details.

Kessler also found that then-current clinical attitudes tended to exaggerate the importance of the penis, with concerns about penis size, and the fear of castration trauma if penectomy were delayed figuring much larger in doctors' deliberations than symmetrical concerns about vaginal size or possible trauma associated with delayed vaginal (re)constructive surgery. Arguably, this is, once again, the

---

10   John Money and Anke Ehrhardt, *Man & Woman, Boy & Girl*.

heritage of Freud, who, as we saw in Chapter 4, saw the vagina as an absence of genitals rather than a genital in its own right.

Among the most worrisome aspects of the treatment approach Kessler's interviewees describe is a general tendency to mislead the patients' parents, and later in life the patients themselves—using white lies and misleading simplifications to convince them their children really are the sex "identified" by the treatment team. Of course, their primary motivation for this dissimulation derived from Money and Ehrhardt's insistence upon the need for parents and loved ones to be completely convinced of an intersex child's reconstructed sex. However, the approach is clearly very deeply at odds with the goal of informed consent.

7.3. Intersex or DSD?

Many of the concerns identified by Kessler are no longer as pressing as they were when she wrote her article. In the early 2000s, intersex activists and clinicians collaborated to produce a new set of intersex treatment guidelines, the "Consensus Statement on Management of Intersex Disorders."[11] Among other things, the new guidelines stipulate that doctors communicate clearly and honestly with patients and their parents about intersex conditions, and that in general surgical options be deferred until patients are old enough to decide for themselves. While these guidelines have not been universally adopted, they have begun to produce improvements for intersex children.

However, the same collaboration that produced these guidelines also resulted in a controversy over nomenclature, a controversy that has driven a wedge into the intersex community. Philosopher Ellen Feder and anthropologist Katrina Karkazis offer a nice summary of that controversy, as well as an argument for Feder and Karkazis's own position, in their 2008 article "What's in a Name: The Controversy over 'Disorders of Sex Development.'"[12] The authors begin by tracing the history of nomenclature associated

---

11   Peter Lee et al., "Consensus Statement on Management of Intersex Disorders," e488-e500.

12   Ellen Feder and Katrina Karkazis, "What's in a Name: The Controversy over 'Disorders of Sex Development,'" 3–36.

with intersex—from "hermaphroditism" and "pseudohermaphrodit-ism" until well into the twentieth century, to "intersex" with the rise of intersex activism and solidarity in the 1990s. They report that unfortunately this usage of "intersex" was controversial, espe-cially to clinicians who wanted to limit the term to clinical usages rather than broader identity categories, and to parents, many of whom were distressed by the suggestion, concordant with the term "intersex," that their children were neither male nor female, or were somehow both. For this reason, some intersex patients too found the term stigmatizing; hence, many doctors avoided using it in their clinical practices, even after it had become the standard term in the medical literature.

In the increasingly used acronym we first encountered for the range of queer identities, "LGBTTIQQ2S," the "I" stands for "Intersex"; and this was sometimes found objectionable because of its connotation of queerness. Not all intersex people feel like, or want to be, part of the queer community. For this reason, even well-intentioned uses of terms like "LGBTTIQQ2S," or symbols like the rainbow flag used in association with intersex people, may carry the danger of misrepresenting the intentions and self-identifications of people they purport to represent.

Ultimately, "Disorder of Sexual Development," or DSD, was adopted as the preferred clinical term. However, many long-time intersex scholars and activists angrily reject the term because it imputes to intersex people a disorder rather than a mere difference. (Indeed, it is for this reason that I continue to use the term "intersex" rather than "DSD," and indeed use it throughout this chapter.)

Feder and Karkazis survey the options, and the reasons for them, before giving their vote to "DSD." While they have long been critics of the medicalization of intersex, the authors argue that the new terminology—unlike both "hermaphrodite" and "intersex"—focuses on the patient's well-being rather than the patient's gender.

Since some intersex conditions will continue to require spe-cialist medical care, there is a pragmatic reason to group them and to name them. Feder and Karkazis maintain that using the same terminology for identity groups associated with gender as for clinical usage inappropriately conflates cultural and medical considerations. In this way, using the term "intersex" in a clinical setting treats intersex as a disorder like no other. The authors write, "Doctors have thereby justified treatment of these conditions in ways that defy accepted medical practice and that violate long-established principles of bioethics."[13] They hope that the terminology of DSD, combined with clinically descriptive terms, will eventuate in a new approach that will instead treat intersex as a disorder like any other.

7.4. Questions for reflection

- Besides intersex, what other types of physical variations occur within human populations? Which of them do we count as "conditions"? Which of them are not pathologized in this way? Why? Is neo-natal surgical treatment as common a response to such cases as to intersex? Why do you think that is?
- During the time Kessler documents, clinicians regarded it as more humane to normalize intersex children by subjecting them to sex reassignment surgery and hormonal treatments than to send them into the world with atypical anatomical features and a potentially complicated gender identity. What do you think? Which of the two alternatives is more in keeping with the classic injunction to physicians "First, do no harm"? Why?
- Imagine that you are a doctor who specializes in intersex children and you genuinely believe Money and Ehrhardt's claim that parents must be totally convinced of a child's sex for the corresponding gender identity to develop naturally. How might you convince parents of their child's sex while still obtaining their informed consent for surgical procedures? Is it possible to balance these two goals? Why or why not?
- Which terminology do you think is most apt: "intersex" or "DSD"? Why? If neither is adequate, can you think of a better alternative?

---

13   Feder and Karkazis, 134.

7.5. Works cited and recommended reading

Blackless, Melanie et al. "How Sexually Dimorphic Are We? Review and Synthesis." *American Journal of Human Biology* 12 (2000): 151–66.

Dreger, Alice. *Hermaphrodites and the Medical Invention of Sex.* Cambridge, MA: Harvard University Press, 1998.

Fausto-Sterling, Anne. "The Five Sexes: Why Male and Female Are Not Enough." *Sciences* (March/April 1993): 20–24.

Feder, Ellen and Katrina Karkazis. "What's in a Name: The Controversy over 'Disorders of Sex Development.'" *Hastings Center Report* 38.5 (2008): 33–36.

Holmes, Morgan. *Intersex: A Perilous Difference.* Selinsgrove, PA: Susquehanna University Press, 2008.

Intersex Society of North America website. <www.isna.org>. Accessed 1 May 2015.

Kessler, Suzanne. "The Medical Construction of Gender: Case Management of Intersexed Infants." *Signs* 16.1 (1990): 3–26.

Lee, Peter et al. "Consensus Statement on Management of Intersex Disorders." *Pediatrics* 118.2 (2006): e488–e500.

Money, John and Anke Ehrhardt. *Man & Woman, Boy & Girl.* Baltimore: Johns Hopkins University Press, 1972.

Sax, L. "How Common Is Intersex? A Response to Anne Fausto-Sterling." *Journal of Sex Research* 39.3 (August 2002): 174–78.

CHAPTER 8

Trans Issues

8.1. What does it mean to be trans?

Last chapter, we discussed intersex people, people whose phenotype or genotype is atypical with respect to sex markers. Sometimes, lay people mistakenly lump intersex people in with trans people. In a way, this confusion is understandable. The existence of both groups destabilizes some of our commonest beliefs about human sex and gender. Moreover, members of both groups often receive similar endocrinological and surgical treatments. As well, unsurprisingly, both intersex people and trans people are often subject to similar prejudices. Despite these commonalities, there is a world of difference between intersex people and trans people. Intersex people are born physically atypical. By contrast, trans people are born physically typical with respect to sex, but develop gender identities that are misaligned with their gender assignment at birth.

In this chapter, we will consider some of the issues faced by people whose gender identity does not match their phenotypic sex. We'll start by getting clear on the terminology—both identity terms and diagnostic terms. As we do so, we'll survey some of the issues and concepts associated with trans identities and with trans people's clinical experiences. From there, we will move on to an examination of the tension between some radical feminists and trans people. We'll conclude the chapter with a short discussion of transphobia and transmisogyny.

8.1.1. Identity terms

As we briefly noted in Chapters 6 and 7, the queer spectrum has come to be associated with a number of long acronyms intended to capture the various queer identities. One version is "LGBTTIQQ2S," which stands for "Lesbian, Gay, Bisexual, Transsexual, Transgender, Intersex, Queer, Questioning, and Two-spirited." It turns out that each of these terms on its own includes a range of different identities. Arguably, none of them gets as confused by people outside of the queer community as "transsexual" and "transgender."

Indeed, "transgender" itself has come to operate as a kind of umbrella term for a range of different sexual identities that in one way or another resist the gender binary. In the broadest terms, to be transgender is for one's gender identity to fail to align with one's gender assignment or phenotypic sex, either because one identifies as the "opposite" sex, or because one's gender identity defies binaristic classification.

> Notice that, in the above passage and in the remainder of this chapter, I use "gender assignment" and "phenotypic sex" more or less interchangeably. We learned about these terms in Chapter 2 and Chapter 7, respectively. Take a moment to think about each of those terms. How would you define them? Given what you've learned so far in this volume, do you think it is appropriate to use these terms as near synonyms? Or, is there a principled basis for disambiguating between them? Which of the terms is more appropriate in this context? Why?

While several of the identities on the queer spectrum involve sexual orientation, this is not the case with trans identities. Just like cisgender people, transgender people can be straight, gay, bisexual, pansexual, or asexual. However, societal norms around sexual orientation—the view, for instance, that real women are sexually attracted to men—have sometimes led to prejudice against non-heterosexual transgender people, and to the accusation that they are not really trans. This is just mistaken. Whether or not one is trans depends not on one's sexual desires, but on one's gender identity and its relation to one's phenotypic sex.

Cisgender

The prefix "cis" is of Latin origin and means "on this side of." It contrasts with "trans," also Latin, meaning "across." In recent years, trans scholars and activists, along with their allies, have begun using the term "cisgender" to describe people whose gender identity accords with their gender assignment or phenotypic sex. This terminological innovation owes a great deal to Beauvoir's diagnosis of the problem of the Other. (See Chapter 4 for a reminder of how this goes.) The use of the "cis-" prefix is meant to render conceptually symmetrical the One/Other relationship between cis and trans people. It is hoped that the use of the term reminds cisgender people of their privilege, and avoids treating transgender people as special cases or exceptions.

For years, "transsexual," as opposed to "transgender," was the usual term for someone who identified as the gender opposite to their sex at birth and who had undergone, or was undergoing, medical interventions to transition to the sex corresponding to their identity. In this context, "MTF" is the short-form for male-to-female transsexual, while "FTM" stands for female-to-male transsexual. However, more recently, trans people have challenged the inappropriate emphasis that others often place on their private medical histories, including details about whether or not they have undergone sex reassignment surgery or "SRS." (Notice that SRS is different from "gender reassignment," a term associated with intersex infants, not transsexual adults. See Chapter 2 for a refresher on the latter term.) Just as one need not be heterosexual to be trans, so one need not undergo SRS or hormone therapy to count as really trans. Moreover, whether or not one has undergone such treatments is a highly personal matter into which other people have no right to enquire. For many trans people, using the more general term "transgender" is a way to resist communicating whether they have undergone, or plan to undergo, SRS. Replacing "MTF" with "trans woman" or "transfeminine," and "FTM" with "trans man" or "transmasculine" similarly averts disclosing private medical information.

Distinct from this, some people identify as "transgender" rather than "transsexual" as a means of further resisting a perceived binarism in some trans experiences. That is, some trans people identify as "transgender" rather than "transsexual" precisely because they straddle the gender binary that is reproduced in identities like "trans man" and "trans woman." They might wear a beard while favouring the pronoun "she," or might use gender-neutral pronouns like "ze" or "hir" instead of "s/he" and "him/her," and so on. "Transgender" in this sense of the term aligns closely with such gender identities as "agender," "gender fluid," and "genderqueer" (not to mention the more radical "genderfuck").

Recently, some trans people and their allies have begun deploying the term "trans*" (note the asterisk) in place of "transgender" in order to signify inclusivity and a broad openness to the full range of trans identities, in particular non-binary trans identities. However, some trans activists and bloggers criticize the use of "trans*." Some of these critics argue that both "transgender" and "trans," unlike "transsexual," are already inclusive in precisely the way that "trans*" is intended to capture. In stark contrast, other critics maintain that the trans community is problematically hierarchical and exclusive, and that signalling inclusivity with "trans*" is therefore misleading.

> In this volume, unless more specificity is required, I refer to all transsexual and transgender people, whether binary or non-binary, as "trans" or "transgender." I adopt this convention both because these terms are today more widely known and used than "trans*" and because, at time of writing, it is not clear whether "trans*" will survive its current contestation.

Pronoun choice poses yet another layer of linguistic complexity when dealing with trans identities. This issue was brought to the fore recently with Olympic athlete and reality television star Caitlyn Jenner's well-publicized transition. When Jenner first revealed in an interview with television journalist Diane Sawyer that she identifies as a woman, she indicated that at that time she still preferred to be referred to with masculine pronouns ("he," "him," etc.). Sawyer and many other reporters used masculine pronouns in accordance with Jenner's wishes, but some bloggers expressed vexation at this choice. Later, when Jenner adopted her new name and feminine pronouns, a number of anti-trans commentators continued to refer to Jenner using masculine pronouns.

Indeed, the phenomenon of intentional "mispronouning" pre-dates the Jenner story. It has for years been a trope for opponents of trans people—these opponents include both social conservatives, and trans-exclusionary feminists (see 8.3 for more on the latter group)—to refer to trans people using the pronouns associated with their gender assignment at birth rather than the pronouns that align with their gender identity. Intentional mispronouning is intended to convey skepticism about the aptness of the new pronouns, and with it a deeper skepticism about the legitimacy of trans identities. The reason that some trans-positive bloggers were anxious about Sawyer's use of masculine pronouns for Jenner is that they worried that Sawyer and others were mispronouning Jenner in just this way.

Even when we do not intend to mispronoun trans people, it can be extremely difficult to know which pronoun to use with someone with a non-binary gender expression. Similarly, it can be difficult to know—or remember—which pronoun to use when a trans person is transitioning, or is only "out" to a few people. Besides, we cannot tell at a glance what anyone's gender identity is. In order to address these challenges, members of queer, feminist, and progressive communities have increasingly taken to including both their names and their preferred pronouns when they introduce themselves: "Hi, I'm Shannon, and I prefer feminine pronouns." Still others, adopt the pronoun "they" (and cognates such as "them" and "their") as a singular gender-neutral pronoun for everyone. While this device can cause occasional confusion with interlocutors who hear "they" as plural, the singular "they" has actually been in use for centuries. More importantly, using it can help prevent trans and gender nonconforming people from feeling hurt or embarrassed. In general, though, a good rule of thumb for pronoun use, as for other types of nomenclature, is to let people decide for themselves what they wish to be called.

What a drag!

Transvestites and drag queens/kings are sometimes mistakenly included under the "transgender" umbrella, but in fact their gender identity (typically) matches their phenotypic sex. That they are sometimes classified as trans is partly owing to nineteenth- and early twentieth-century conflations of various "non-standard" gender expressions by scholars like Ulrichs (see Chapter 5 for a reminder of Ulrichs's views), but also because of confused (or just plain transphobic) characterizations of trans people as men in women's clothing or vice versa. Typically, however, transvestites derive pleasure from cross-dressing even though their gender identities align with their gender assignments; likewise, most drag kings/queens are cisgender people who simply enjoy participating in this distinctive genre of gender-bending performance.

Drag shows in large part treat gender as a fluid category with which we can play and be creative. However, for many trans people, actually being able to live as the gender with which they identify is a serious, consequential matter, and not the site of playfulness. Moreover, drag performance often trades in over-the-top stereotypes about gender (and gender-bending), stereotypes many trans people find harmful. One culturally prominent example of this can be found in the popular Broadway musical, *Hedwig and the Angry Inch*, and in the film based upon that musical. In those productions, the protagonist, Hedwig, a trans woman, is represented as unstable, capricious, selfish, and ultimately "really" male. While *Hedwig* is ostensibly about a trans character, the musical actually originated as a drag show in New York's gay community. It is perhaps unsurprising that in its representation of its protagonist, the musical retains and reproduces drag stereotypes.

8.2. Diagnostic terms

Psychiatrists and psychologists played a major role in twentieth-century trans history, and continue in the twenty-first century to play a large role. Historically, psychiatrists and psychologists pathologized trans identities, and played gatekeeper roles for trans people seeking hormonal or surgical intervention. While the latter remains true today, the former shifted dramatically in 2013.

Until 2013, the American Psychiatric Association (APA) regarded transgenderism as one of a pair of mental illnesses, GID (Gender Identity Disorder) and GIDC (Gender Identity Disorder—Child). The main difference between the two conditions was whether "symptoms" present in childhood or adulthood. The four criteria for a diagnosis of GID are as follows:

- Strong and persistent cross-gender identification,
- Persistent discomfort about one's assigned sex or a sense of inappropriateness in the gender-role of that sex,
- Absence of a concurrent physical intersex condition,
- Clinically significant distress or impairment in social, occupational, or other important areas of functioning.[1]

Understandably, many trans people resented the claim that transgenderism is a mental illness. However, in many jurisdictions, they were forced to obtain a psychiatric diagnosis of GID in order to obtain sex reassignment surgery. Indeed, many trans people who have successfully navigated the mental health system in order to obtain surgery provide detailed advice to pre-op trans people on how to answer psychiatrists' questions "correctly" in order to receive the desired diagnosis. Arguably, therefore, psychiatrists retained a very narrow, and potentially inaccurate, sense of the ways in which transgenderism manifests since all or most of their patients follow the same DSM-inspired script.

Our conception of what counts as a mental illness is an evolving social construct. For instance, in the nineteenth century, psychologists regarded African-American slaves' desire to escape from servitude as a form of mental illness, which they termed "drapetomania." Similarly, until 1973, mainstream psychologists and psychiatrists

---

1   Diagnostic criteria for these conditions are described in detail in the APA's *Diagnostic and Statistical Manual of Mental Disorders*, Edition 4 TR ("TR" stands for "Text Revision").

regarded homosexuality as a form of mental illness. Today, some clinicians continue to regard homosexuality as a mental illness, curable through, for instance, "conversion therapy." However, these therapists for the most part occupy the fringes of mainstream psychology and psychiatry.

In 2013, the APA published the fifth edition of its statistical manual, the DSM-5. In preparation for this new edition, there was considerable research and lobbying by various groups (both trans activists and allies, and groups that are anything but allies) about what diagnostic terms, if any, that edition should include for transgenderism. Socially conservative lobbyists, many of them affiliated with religious groups, urged the view that trans identity is a kind of psychosis, and moreover that it is medically irresponsible to "mutilate" psychotic patients by performing sex reassignment surgery on them. Conversely, those advocating for trans people objected to treating trans identity in itself as a diagnosable condition, but worried that altogether excising mention of trans identities from the DSM might make it difficult for trans people to receive health insurance, sick leave, and other supports if they choose to undergo sex reassignment surgery. The version of the DSM-5 that was eventually published aligns closely with the concerns of these trans advocates.

> Here is the URL for a useful one-pager the APA released to explain its latest diagnostic approach to gender dysphoria: <http://www.dsm5.org/documents/gender%20dysphoria%20fact%20sheet.pdf>.

In the new manual, "Gender Identity Disorder" has been replaced by "Gender Dysphoria." The new nomenclature is intended to signal that having a gender identity that does not align with one's gender assignment is not in itself a disorder. What makes it a diagnosable condition is the "clinically significant distress" associated with the misalignment. ("Dysphoria" comes from the Greek word "dusphoros" which means "hard to bear.") Under the new system, a trans person who does not experience distress because of their trans identity is not regarded as mentally ill. As with the DSM-4-TR, the DSM-5 distinguishes between adult and pediatric versions of the condition, the main force of that distinction being that, according to the APA, children with gender dysphoria often outgrow the condition, unlike adults, who do not. Finally, the new manual includes a specification that, post-transition, patients who are no longer experiencing clinically significant distress may still receive ongoing treatment under the rubric of gender dysphoria.

In this chapter, you have been introduced in broad strokes to the history of terminology and psychiatric diagnoses that have been associated with trans people. If you wish to learn more about the history of trans identities, you may enjoy reading Patrick Califia's overview of the autobiographies of trans pioneers like Christine Jorgensen, Mario Martino, and Jan Morris.[2] Or, you may prefer to read those autobiographies for yourself. They are all listed in the "Works cited and recommended reading" section below.

When you read about early trans people's experiences, two things become salient. The first is that, for trans people, the decision to transition and to live openly as the gender that aligns with their gender identity is a very serious, and frequently difficult, commitment made after long consideration. While popular television shows like *South Park* and *Family Guy* unfortunately help to sustain the myth of the capricious trans person, that myth is remote from the real experiences of trans people.

Second, for Jorgensen, Morris, and Martino, doctors and psychologists served a crucial gatekeeper function. While both Jorgensen and Morris regarded their clinicians with warm affection and gratitude—Jorgensen even went so far as adopting her post-transition forename from her surgeon's name—Martino had no love lost for his often unhelpful, and sometimes harmful, doctors.

As the debates over the DSM make clear, doctors continue to wield considerable power as gatekeepers for trans people. Harry Benjamin was a mid-twentieth-century German-American endocrinologist who was an important early advocate of the view that gender dysphoria was more appropriately "treated" by sex reassignment surgery than by psychoanalysis. His ground-breaking book, *The Transsexual Phenomenon*, is also listed below.

---

2   Patrick Califia, "Transsexual Autobiography: The First Wave," 11–51.

8.3. Trans identities, radical feminism, and women-only spaces

One of the most painful disagreements to emerge in recent decades is that between some radical feminists and trans people. Emerging in the 1960s, radical feminism as a movement was (and still is) organized around the idea that the patriarchy constitutes the underlying structure of society. In other words, for radical feminists, the organization of power, authority, and goods in society—indeed, in all societies—serves to privilege men and to disadvantage women. One important proponent of this view was Shulamith Firestone, who held that all social hierarchies are modelled on the gender hierarchy. (We'll look at Firestone's ideas a bit more closely in Chapter 9.) While not all radical feminists agree with Firestone that the gender hierarchy is more fundamental than, say, racial or class hierarchies, all radical feminists regard the gender hierarchy as ubiquitous, systemic, and deeply unjust. Indeed, for radical feminists, patriarchy is so deeply entrenched in our social institutions that those institutions are not susceptible of reform. It is for this reason that they propose two very different radical solutions—on the one hand, the eradication of gender, and on the other, separatist feminism. Unfortunately, whether intentionally or not, both of these approaches end up marginalizing trans people.

8.3.1. Abolishing gender

For Firestone-inspired radical feminists, the so-called *gender binary*—the view that there are two and only two genders, and that everyone belongs to one and only one of them—is a patriarchal construct that systemically disadvantages those marked by the construct as female.

Philosopher Sally Haslanger puts it this way: "for most of us there is a relatively fixed interpretation of our bodies as sexed either male or female, an interpretation that marks us within the dominant ideology as eligible for only certain positions or opportunities in a system of sexist oppression."[3] Because, on her account, gender

---

3   Sally Haslanger, "Gender and Race: (What) Are They? (What) Do We Want Them to Be?," 42.

categories really do serve to give power to, or withhold power from, those so-categorized, Haslanger offers definitions of "woman" and "man" that make specific reference to women's and men's places within systems of power. Here is Haslanger's definition of "woman":

> S *is a woman* iff [if and only if]
> i.   S is regularly and for the most part observed or imagined to have certain bodily features presumed to be evidence of a female's biological role in reproduction;
> ii. that S has these features marks S within the dominant ideology of S's society as someone who ought to occupy certain kinds of social position that are in fact subordinate (and so motivates and justifies S's occupying such a position); and
> iii. the fact that S satisfies (i) and (ii) plays a role in S's systematic subordination, i.e., *along some dimension*, S's social position is oppressive, and S's satisfying (i) and (ii) plays a role in that dimension of subordination.[4]

On this understanding, oppression and injustice are part of the very constitution of gender, not merely a contingent effect of gender divisions. If this view is right, then gender cannot be reformed, and ought to be eradicated. Recall Overall's plea, mentioned in Chapter 2, to "junk gender."

Feminists who advocate for the eradication of gender are at the opposite end of the continuum from feminist essentialists. (We looked at Irigaray's feminist essentialism in Chapter 4. We'll briefly revisit feminist essentialism in Chapter 11.) Feminist essentialists argue that there really are distinct masculine and feminine ways of being in the world, and that we ought to embrace the latter. By contrast, those radical feminists who support the abolition of gender regard gender differences as socially constructed, and resist them on all axes. That is, they reject gender divisions of labour, gendered conventions around attire, grooming, and behaviour, etc.

Such feminists sometimes express frustration with trans people, and in particular with trans women, for allegedly reinforcing gender stereotypes. For instance, after Caitlyn Jenner's famous *Vanity Fair*

---

4   Haslanger, 42.

cover, in which she was pictured with make-up and well-coiffed hair and wearing a corset, feminist author and Academy Award winning film-maker Elinor Burkett published an opinion piece[5] in the *New York Times* in which she argued that Jenner's embrace of traditional feminine gender roles (these range from feeling more in touch with her emotions to wearing nail polish) flies in the face of feminists' decades-long effort to dissolve those very gender roles. The article struck a nerve among both radical feminists and transfeminists. The result was a major dust-up in the feminist blogosphere, in the context of which some bloggers accused Burkett of transphobia, and others defended her view.

Some radical feminist criticisms have gone beyond merely complaining about trans people's alleged reinforcement of traditional gender roles. One common radical feminist trope is to accuse trans people of having "mutilated" themselves by undergoing sex reassignment surgery. It would be better, they argue, to work to abolish gender, or to develop a more fluid notion of gender detached from anatomical features, than to mutilate oneself in order to conform to conservative ideas about gender.

Having gotten this far in the volume, you may well find the radical feminist opposition to gender roles, and indeed to gender, quite plausible. However, the accusation of mutilation is clearly a hurtful one for trans people (and seems as if it is intended to be so). Moreover, many trans people argue that it is "cis privilege" that makes opposition to gender possible. Cis feminists, they maintain, have never had to defend their gender identity or to fight to express it. This allows them to be cavalier about gender, treating it as if it were dispensable. For trans people, who lack this kind of privilege, their gender identity is often at the core of their self-identity. Thus, they have no interest in eradicating it.

8.3.2. Women-only spaces

While some radical feminists support the eradication of gender, others advocate instead (or in the meantime) for the separation of the genders. Separatist feminists, including lesbian separatists

---

5   Elinor Burkett, "What Makes a Woman?," *New York Times*, 6 June 2015.

(discussed briefly in Chapter 4), regard women-only spaces as the best response to the patriarchal structure of mainstream society. On the view of feminist separatists, men, men's desires, and men's systems of power so thoroughly dominate society that women can only hope to escape that power by isolating themselves from it. Thus, separatist feminists both seek to avoid interactions with men (and with women who have not separated themselves from men) and to work to create women-only spaces. While some women-only spaces (Take Back the Night marches, for instances, or university women's centres) welcome trans people, others do not.

Those separatist feminists and separatist feminist organizations that exclude trans people do so on several grounds. They regard trans men as having abandoned their female identity in order to pursue male privilege. By contrast, they often regard trans women as still infected with the male privilege with which they grew up. "Women-born-women," they argue, have distinct experiences as a result of having grown up embodied female and socialized as women, that socialization including having been subject to masculine privilege. Trans women, they maintain, cannot understand what it is like to have grown up as a member of the subordinate gender. Less commonly, some separatist feminists accuse trans women of having adopted feminine gender identities precisely in order to infiltrate women-only spaces.

Perhaps the most notorious example of a separatist feminist institution that excludes trans women is the Michigan Womyn's Music Festival,[6] or Michfest, a lesbian feminist music festival held annually from 1976 to 2015 (its last year). While some trans people always attended the festival, they had to do so discreetly since the festival was officially intended exclusively for "womyn-born-womyn." Over the years, there were a number of well-publicized expulsions of trans women from the festival. These expulsions led to a campaign by Equality Michigan to convince Michfest organizers to change the festival's policy in order to include trans people.

6   The modified spelling here eliminates "man" and "men" in the words "woman" and "women" and represents the rejection of traditions that define woman by reference to the male norm.

The exclusion of trans people by radical feminists led to trans-activists' coining of the term *TERF*, or *trans-exclusionary radical feminism*, a term that so-called TERFs themselves reject. It is important to note that not all radical feminists reject trans people and their experiences. Moreover, many transfeminists are importantly influenced by some of the ideas at the heart of radical feminism. Nonetheless, the disagreement between some radical feminists and transfeminists is deep and extremely divisive, and is likely to continue for the foreseeable future.

Transphobia and trans-misogyny

The increasing media visibility of trans people like Laverne Cox and Caitlyn Jenner means that many members of the public are today much better informed about trans identities than they were even a decade ago. However, trans identities remain among the most stigmatized. Indeed, it is still common for television programs such as *Family Guy*, *Bob's Burgers*, and *Big Bang Theory* to make unkind jokes at the expense of trans people, jokes that would today be unthinkable if directed at gays or lesbians, or at members of ethnic minorities. More seriously, trans people are disproportionately the victims of violence, harassment, and discrimination. Trans people of colour experience even higher rates of such harms. In short, transphobia remains endemic.[7]

Moreover, trans scholar, author, and activist Julia Serano argues that trans women and transfeminine people experience not only transphobia but also trans-misogyny. "Trans-misogyny" is Serano's term for a particular kind of hatred at the intersection of misogyny (the hatred of women) and transphobia (the fear of trans people). To direct trans-misogyny at someone is to hate them doubly, both for being trans and for exemplifying feminine traits. In her useful primer on the concept, Serano writes that "individuals on the trans female/feminine spectrum are culturally marked, not for failing to conform to gender norms per se, but because of the specific

---

7   For some recent statistics on discrimination against trans people, see Jaime Grant et al., *Injustice at Every Turn: A Report of the National Transgender Discrimination Survey*.

direction of their gender transgression—that is, because of their feminine gender expression and/or their female gender identities. Thus, the marginalization of trans female/feminine spectrum people is not merely a result of transphobia, but is better described as trans-misogyny. Trans-misogyny is steeped in the assumption that femaleness and femininity are inferior to, and exist primarily for the benefit of, maleness and masculinity."[8]

Remember our Chapter 2 discussion of intersectionality? Serano's identification of the phenomenon of trans-misogyny is intersectional analysis in action.

8.4. Questions for reflection

- What do you think about the "cis-" prefix? Is it helpful? Why or why not?
- Are some mental illnesses natural, as opposed to socially constructed? How might we discern "real" mental illnesses from ways of being that are wrongly pathologized in order to reinforce social norms?
- Do you think there is any way to balance radical feminists' opposition to gender binarism with trans people's hard-won right to their preferred gender expression?
- What do you think about women-only spaces? Are they appropriate? For music festivals? For protest marches? For rape shelters? Is there any reason to limit such spaces to cis-women?

8.5. Works cited and recommended reading

American Psychiatric Association. *Diagnostic and Statistical Manual of Mental Disorders: DSM-5*. Arlington, VA: American Psychiatric Publishing, 2013.
——. *Gender Dysphoria*. 2013. <http://www.dsm5.org/ documents/gender%20dysphoria%20fact%20sheet.pdf>. Accessed 3 May 2015.

---

8   Julia Serano, "Trans-misogyny Primer," on the Julia Serano website.

Benjamin, Harry. *The Transsexual Phenomenon*. New York: Julian Press, 1966.

Burkett, Elinor. "What Makes a Woman?" *New York Times*, online edition. 6 June 2015. <http://www.nytimes.com/2015/06/07/opinion/sunday/what-makes-a-woman.html?_r=0>. Accessed 10 June 2015.

Califia, Patrick. "Transsexual Autobiography: The First Wave." *Sex Changes: Transgender Politics*. 2nd ed. Berkeley: Cleis Press, 2003.

Grant, Jaime et al. *Injustice at Every Turn: A Report of the National Transgender Discrimination Survey*. Washington, DC: The National Gay and Lesbian Task Force and the National Center for Transgender Equality, 2011. <http://www.transequality.org/sites/default/files/docs/resources/NTDS_Report.pdf>. Accessed 3 June 2015.

Haslanger, Sally. "Gender and Race: (What) Are They? (What) Do We Want Them to Be?" *Noûs* 34.1 (2000): 31–55.

Jorgensen, Christine. *Christine Jorgensen: A Personal Autobiography*. New York: Bantam, 1967.

Martino, Mario. *Emergence: A Transsexual Autobiography*. New York: Crown Publishers, 1977.

Morris, Jan. *Conundrum*. New York: Harcourt, Brace, Jovanovich, 1974.

Serano, Julia. *Whipping Girl: A Transsexual Woman on Sexism and the Scapegoating of Femininity*. Emeryville, CA: Seal Press, 2007.

———. "Trans-misogyny Primer." N.d. Julia Serano website. <http://www.juliaserano.com/av/TransmisogynyPrimer-Serano.pdf>. Accessed 3 June 2015.

CHAPTER 9

Biodeterminism

9.1. Is biology destiny?

A number of texts in the preceding chapters have suggested in subtle and not-so-subtle ways that important aspects of human gender— perhaps human genders themselves—are socially constructed. In this chapter, we look at the opposite view, namely, that gender is biologically determined. This view is an example of a more general position known as "biodeterminism."

The idea of biodeterminism is most pithily captured by the familiar saying, "biology is destiny." Biodeterminists think that human behaviour is best understood as the result of human beings' innate biological tendencies. Biodeterminism of one stripe or another is very often deployed to explain differences between masculine and feminine gender roles. If someone says that women tend to pursue caring professions because they are naturally more nurturing than men, they are invoking biodeterminism, as does someone who says that women *ought to* pursue caring professions because they are naturally more nurturing than men. Notice the difference between these two claims, though. The first claim is descriptive and seeks merely to explain some aspect of human behaviour. The latter claim, however, is normative, and seeks to affect human conduct.

The second of these claims is an instance of what philosophers call *the naturalistic fallacy*. This is the name for the error in reasoning of which we are guilty when we infer that something is good or bad because it is natural (or from other supposed descriptive facts). When moralists in times past declaimed against "unnatural" sex acts, they were committing the naturalistic fallacy. (They were also probably wrong about the sex acts being unnatural. Most sex acts that human beings perform also occur among other species, but that's another story.)

In this chapter, we will look at some of the most prominent biodeterministic accounts of both sex and gender differences—Darwin's theory of sexual selection, evolutionary psychology, and brain sex theory—as well as some feminist critiques of all three in order to consider the question whether biology is destiny when it comes to sex and gender.

9.2. Darwin on the evolution of sex

Darwin's most famous and important contribution to evolutionary theory was, of course, his *Origin of Species*. There he describes what he terms "natural selection" in the following way. When organisms reproduce, there are occasional chance variations that result in differences between the parent(s) and offspring. When this happens, there are three possible consequences. If the new trait makes the offspring less fit for the econiche it occupies than its parents, it will, on average, have a shorter lifespan than them, and will consequently have a lower chance of itself reproducing and passing on its mutation to offspring. Thus, such traits have a reduced chance of taking hold in a population. If the new trait neither advantages nor disadvantages the offspring relative to its parents, then on average the offspring will live about as long as them and reproduce about as successfully as them. So, the mutation may occur in its offspring, and perhaps in their offspring, etc. Such a neither-harmful-nor-helpful mutation will, then, occasionally recur in the broader population, but is not likely to become a common trait in the species. Finally, a chance variation that better fits an individual to its environment than its parents will on average extend the life of the offspring, and allow it to reproduce with greater success than its parents and other members of the population. This reproductive success will lead to more members of the species acquiring the new trait, such that it becomes common within the species. Over time, enough adaptations of this type lead to the emergence of whole new species.

While natural selection offers an elegant explanation of species change, Darwin was for many years at a loss to explain the emergence of sex differences. It was not until his later *Descent of Man* that he offered an account of why males and females differ from each other. The new mechanism he describes there as a supplement to natural selection is "sexual selection."

Why sex?

Why do species reproduce sexually at all? The ability to reproduce sexually, it turns out, is itself a naturally selected trait. Populations that reproduce sexually have a survival advantage over other populations because the way they recombine genetic material makes them more robust.

Let's imagine that human beings reproduced parthenogenetically—that is, using the genetic material of only one parent. If your (one!) parent had a genetic predisposition to some disease, then so would you. However, since human beings reproduce sexually, if one of your parents has such a genetic predisposition, there is no guarantee you will acquire it since your DNA contains genetic material from both parents. Sexual reproduction results in more varied, and hence more adaptable, populations. Notice, however, that where the choice of sexual partners is extremely limited for a number of generations, such robustness can suffer. That is why some geographically isolated populations often have very high rates of genetic conditions that occur at a lower frequency in the rest of the human population.

Darwin arrived at the question of sex differences indirectly. Before it occurred to him to ask why males and females are different—indeed, why there are males and females at all—he was first at pains to explain why some traits that make their possessors more

vulnerable to predators are nonetheless selected within a population. The bright red feathers of a cardinal, for instance, or the tail
of a peacock, make the bearer more visible to potential enemies.
In the case of the peacock, the tail inhibits escape. On the face of
it such traits should fall into the disadvantageous category and
thus disappear from populations in comparatively short order. The
existence of such traits seems to fly in the face of natural selection.

Of course, as Darwin soon realized, it is not all cardinals who
are red or all peacocks who sport large, brightly coloured tails.
Both of these traits are limited to the males of the species. It was
this realization that led to Darwin's formulation of sexual selection.

Recall that the core mechanism within the process of natural
selection is the ability to produce offspring. An animal that has a
shorter lifespan than other members of its species is on the whole
less likely to produce offspring—and hence pass on its genetic material—than other members of its species. Thus, all other things being
equal, if red feathers make cardinals more vulnerable to predators,
we should expect to see fewer cardinals with red feathers. That is,
unless the red feathers make it easier for the cardinal to achieve
sexual success in the time available to it within its lifespan. This
was the solution to Darwin's problem. If you want to increase your
odds of winning a lottery, you can buy one ticket at a time for many,
many years. Or you can buy a large quantity of tickets all at once.
Whereas natural selection is concerned with the purchase of tickets
in the reproductive lottery *over* time, sexual selection emphasizes
the purchase of such tickets *at* a time. What sorts of mechanisms
allow organisms to make bulk purchases of reproductive lottery
tickets? Or, dropping the lottery analogy, what sort of mechanisms
serve to increase an individual's chances of reproductive success
at a given time?

According to Darwin, sexually selected traits like colourful
plumage derive from one of two kinds of sexual competition: (1)
between individuals of the same sex to drive away or kill their
sexual rivals, (2) between individuals of the same sex to impress
their prospective mate(s). Antlers are an example of the first type
of sexually selected trait. Bucks within ungulate species fight each
other for the chance to mate with females within the population. Of
course, the beautiful tail feathers of the peacock are an example of

the second type of trait: one that appeals to mating females rather than warding off other males.

Notice that antlers pose less of an explanatory challenge for Darwin than do red feathers since antlers may be used to fight off not only rival males of one's own species, but also predators from different species. Unsurprisingly, many biologists think that some traits, like antlers, may be both sexually and naturally selected. If antlers help to fight off predators, does it even make sense to think of them as sexually selected?

Indeed it does. After all, natural selection alone cannot account for the fact that in many species of ungulates the males alone have antlers. If the antlers evolved merely as a means of self-defence against predators, then we would expect to see females with antlers too. This is why sexual selection is an explanation not only for traits that imperil their bearers but also for sexual dimorphism.

The emphasis on warding off other males helps us to think of the difference between natural and sexual selection in a different way than above. Whereas naturally selected traits allow all members of a population to better compete with members of other populations within a particular econiche, sexually selected traits allow individual males within a particular population to better compete with other males in the group. In Darwin's words,

> Sexual selection depends on the success of certain individuals over others of the same sex in relation to the propagation of the species; whilst natural selection depends on the success of both sexes, at all ages, in relation to the general conditions of life.[1]

Having posited sexual selection, Darwin now derives some generalizations about it. First, he observes that sexual dimorphism is more prevalent in the "higher species" than in the lower ones. Moreover, he maintains, among almost all sexually dimorphic species, the dimorphism follows similar patterns:

---

1   Charles Darwin, *Descent of Man, and Selection in Relation to Sex*, 398.

With mammals, birds, reptiles, fishes, insects, and even crusta-
ceans, the differences between the sexes follow almost exactly
the same rules. The males are almost always the wooers; and
they alone are armed with special weapons for fighting with their
rivals. They are generally stronger and larger than the females,
and are endowed with the requisite qualities of courage and
pugnacity. They are provided, either exclusively or in a much
higher degree than the females, with organs for producing vocal
or instrumental music, and with odoriferous glands....[2]

On Darwin's account, both males and females of even highly dimorphic species typically resemble the adult female during their juvenile
period. It is only as they approach mating age that the males of
these species begin to manifest their distinctive sexually selected
traits. Thus, for instance, juvenile male deer have no antlers and
juvenile male lions have no manes.

Although we have in this chapter focused on Darwin's biodeterminism, Darwin himself was also well aware of the ways in which
culture could affect biology. Many of the populations he discusses
in *Descent of Man* are domesticated species, whose desired traits
breeders had by then long known how to cultivate through selective pairing. Darwin writes,

It seems to me almost certain that if the individuals of one sex
were during a long series of generations to prefer pairing with
certain individuals of the other sex, characterised in some peculiar
manner, the offspring would slowly but surely become modified
in this same manner.[3]

It is easy to see how this applies to human populations. If many
generations of human beings sought partners with certain culturally endorsed traits, those traits would begin to proliferate within
the population. By the same token, suppression of the reproductive
opportunities of those lacking the endorsed traits would further
lend to the traits' proliferation. This, of course, is the basis of the

---

2   Darwin, 397.
3   Darwin, 399–400.

notorious practice of eugenics. It is also at the heart of some discouragingly racist and classist remarks Darwin makes in the context of his discussion of sexual selection.

Darwin and Aristotle

There are some obvious similarities between Darwin's and Aristotle's views on sex. Both men rank sexually dimorphic species as the "highest." As well, both of them seem to regard adult females as undeveloped in some respects. For Aristotle, the female is undeveloped in the sense that, due to her father's failure to "prevail" in mating (see Chapter 3 for a reminder of what this means), she fails to fully resemble him. She does not quite attain to the paternal form that is the standard for all offspring. For Darwin, the adult female is undeveloped in the sense that juveniles of both sexes resemble her, but they do not resemble the adult male who came to acquire distinctive traits in adulthood. Can you discern other similarities between Darwin and Aristotle? Any differences? What are they?

9.3 Feminist critiques of Darwin

Although Darwin sought to provide a neutral, solely biological account of evolution, for some decades, critics have charged that his science bears the traces of the social mores of nineteenth-century England. Feminist biologist Ruth Hubbard argues that Darwin's description of typical male and female traits reflects Victorian English mores more than it does real facts of nature. He characterizes males as the more important sex in sexual selection because men were then regarded as the more important gender in human society. Likewise, argue the critics, Darwin reflects prevalent attitudes towards men and women when he represents males as active, aggressive, and sexually appetitive, and females as passive and distinguished only by their aesthetic judgment.

One of the best known feminist responses to Darwin is Elaine Morgan's 1972 book *The Descent of Woman*. In that volume, Morgan, a writer, broadcaster, and popular scientist, expresses her frustration with the inattention Darwin and those evolutionary biologists who followed him pay to the role of females in evolution. In general, Morgan charges, evolutionary biologists primarily attend to male organisms and those traits conventionally associated with male organisms, only calling females in from off-stage when the discussion turns to sex and reproduction.[4] On Morgan's account, this bias on the part of scientists has led to a neglect of evidence that could help us to better understand evolution. Seeking to redress this damage, Morgan develops her own account of human evolution centred on such female-associated tasks as child-bearing and lactation rather than around hunting and tool use. Such a shift in perspective, Morgan argues (we won't rehearse that argument here), suggests the possibility that human beings' ancient ancestors spent a great deal of their time in the water. Morgan's popularization of the so-called Aquatic Ape Hypothesis met with considerable skepticism in scientific quarters and was never seriously taken up, but it captured the imagination of the popular readership and offered a glimpse of a female-centred evolutionary biology.

Another hugely influential feminist criticism of mainstream evolutionary biology is Ruth Hubbard's "Have Only Men Evolved?" In it, Hubbard excoriates Darwin for his anthropomorphic descriptions of non-human animals:

> Some might argue in defense of Darwin that the bees (or birds or what have you) do act that way. But the language Darwin uses to describe these behaviours disqualifies him as an objective observer. His animals are cast into roles from a Victorian script. And whereas no one can claim to have solved the important methodological questions of how to disembarrass oneself of one's anthropocentric and cultural biases when observing animal behaviour, surely one must begin by trying.[5]

Hubbard alleges that in his account of sexual selection, Darwin reproduces social gender norms because of the way he allows himself to fall into anthropocentrism. Moreover, she agrees with Morgan that Darwin pays much closer attention to males than to females.

---

4   Elaine Morgan, *The Descent of Woman*, 3–4.
5   Ruth Hubbard, "Have Only Men Evolved?," 94.

Thus, she argues, Darwin's evolutionary theory is not only anthropocentric, but *androcentric*. "*The Descent of Man*," she writes, "is quite literally *his* journey."[6]

She further faults evolutionary theorists post-Darwin for their tendency to engage in speculation about the lives of our distant ancestors. In response to one biologist's description of prehistoric males learning tool use from their fathers, Hubbard quips, "It seems a remarkable feat of clairvoyance to see in such detail what happened some two hundred fifty thousand years in pre-history, complete with the little boy and his little stone chipping set just like daddy's big one."[7]

Hubbard also criticizes evolutionary anthropologists for their reliance on analogies between human beings and non-human primates. Such an approach, Hubbard argues, seems to suggest that in observing other primates, we are observing our own ancestors. However, she cautions, we did not descend from modern apes. Indeed, today's non-human primates are themselves the descendants of earlier species. To forget this fact, she suggests, is once again to forget that men are not the only ones who evolved:

> Most scientists find it convenient to forget that present-day apes and monkeys have had as long an evolutionary history as human beings have had, since the time we went our separate ways. There is no theoretical reason why their behaviour should tell us more about our ancestry than our behaviour tells us about theirs. But just as in the androcentric paradigm men evolved while women cheered from the bleachers, so in the anthropocentric one humans evolved while the apes watched from the trees.[8]

In the end, Hubbard agrees with Morgan that scientists' disproportionate attention to the evolution of males has led to a distorted account of human evolution. She alleges in particular that evolutionary anthropologists overemphasize tool use and hunting and underemphasize language and speech. She reports that scientists'

---

6   Hubbard, 94.
7   Hubbard, 103.
8   Hubbard, 106.

fascination with the traditionally male domains of tool use and hunting led them to the implausible view that language evolved in tandem with the development of tool use and hunting practices. Hubbard dismisses this view on the basis that the development of speech required changes to human physiology, especially to the face and larynx, that could not have happened as quickly as the emergence of tool use and group hunting practices. Hubbard argues that scientists overemphasize tool use and hunting precisely because they regard them as masculine practices. The same, however, cannot be said for speech. After all, Hubbard tells us, "No one ever claimed that women cannot talk."[9]

9.4. Darwin's descendants: Evolutionary psychology and brain sex

9.4.1. Evolutionary psychology

Morgan's and Hubbard's criticisms are primarily directed against biologists, and to some extent, anthropologists. However, in recent years, a new group of scholars has joined the debate on human evolution. *Evolutionary psychologists* seek to apply evolutionary explanations to psychological phenomena. Thus, for instance, an evolutionary psychologist might explain some aspect of human sense perception by arguing that this trait was adaptive for our ancestors.

In a range of ways, evolutionary psychologists very often take the view that gendered differences in behaviour are the product of natural selection. David Buss, for instance, argues that many gender differences among humans are attributable to the different adaptive demands placed on modern humans' ancestors. Members of both sexes had to be able to adapt to high temperatures, he argues; therefore, both sexes have sweat glands. By contrast, only females had to give birth; so, only females have dilating cervices. The same principle, he argues, apply to psychological differences.

> To an evolutionary psychologist, the likelihood that the sexes are psychologically identical in domains in which they have

---

9   Hubbard, 106.

recurrently confronted different adaptive problems over the long expanse of human evolutionary history is essentially zero.... The key question, therefore, is not whether men and women differ psychologically. Rather, the key questions about sex differences, from an evolutionary psychological perspective, are (a) In what domains have women and men faced different adaptive problems? (b) What are the sex-differentiated psychological mechanisms of women and men that have evolved in response to these sex-differentiated adaptive problems? (c) Which social, cultural, and contextual inputs moderate the magnitude of expressed sex differences?[10]

On Buss's account, differences in adaptive demands on humans' evolutionary forebears resulted in the following modern differences between men and women: men enjoy casual sex more than women do, women are more selective about short-term romantic partners than men are, women more than men are attracted to prospective partners with material wealth and ambition, and men are more distressed by sexual infidelity than emotional infidelity whilst the converse is true for women.

In 2002, evolutionary psychology achieved a sudden public prominence with the release of Steven Pinker's best-selling book *The Blank Slate: The Modern Denial of Human Nature*. In it, Pinker deploys evolutionary biology, neuroscience, and cognitive science to attack social constructivism, including social constructivism about gender. He dismisses social constructivism about gender as "gender feminism," a view he regards as at-odds with scientific evidence and good sense. Pinker's discussion of gender feminism is superficial and laden with unnecessary invective. However, the catalogue of evidence he adduces against gender feminism serves as a useful primer on biodeterministic accounts of gender.

Work like Buss's helped to launch a new growth area in evolutionary psychological accounts of gender. Male aggression—including, notoriously, rape—we are told, is the result of evolution, as is

---

10   David Buss, "Psychological Sex Differences: Origins Through Sexual Selection," 164.

the shortage of women in math and engineering. Unsurprisingly, feminist scholars very often take a dim view of this line of argument. If you are committed from the outset of your inquiry to the idea that there are innate gender differences, they argue, then you will no doubt find such differences, and find an evolutionary story to explain them. However, this is just confirmation bias (the search for, or interpretation of, information in a way that confirms one's preconceptions) and does not provide independent evidence of gender differences. Moreover, that evolutionary story is, as Hubbard points out, necessarily speculative. We do not have direct evidence of what the lives of our ancestors were like. While some evolutionary psychologists use the behaviour of today's non-human animals as an analogy for our ancestors' behaviour, there is no guarantee that our ancestors behaved in this way. Indeed, some of the observed animal behaviours should not even be generalized to their whole species. Some evolutionary psychologists, for instance, draw inferences about rape among humans from observations of rape in captive duck populations. However, feminist critics reply that this is tantamount to generalizing from prison rape to rape in the whole human race. When they are kept in captivity, organisms often behave in ways that are not typical of their species. Finally, even if the psychological gender differences discussed by evolutionary psychologists actually obtain, it is difficult, if not impossible, to control for social origins of these differences. For instance, even if it were the case that women disproportionately prefer materially wealthy mates, this is surely an understandable preference for women, given that, on average, they earn a fraction of what men do. Put differently: if our society is so constituted that women typically earn much less money than men, then some women's preference for wealthy mates might be a matter of prudence rather than one of genetics.

9.4.2. Brain sex and its critics

The debate between feminist science scholars and those evolutionary psychologists who argue that gender differences are innate is reproduced in microcosm in the brain sex debate. In recent years, neuroscientist Simon Baron-Cohen has famously argued that

differences in male and female neurophysiology result in differences in the expression of male and female intelligence. Men, he
argues, are in general systemizers, while women are empathizers.
Put differently, men's very brain function inclines them to sort and
organize data, while women's makes them care more for other
people. Baron-Cohen is quick to point out that these differences
hold at the level of whole populations, but not necessarily for all
individuals. Thus, on his view, some men are empathizers and some
women are systemizers, even though this is not typical of the whole
species. Baron-Cohen has achieved particular prominence for his
"extreme male brain" theory, his hypothesis that there are crucial
neurological and psychometric similarities between the most highly
systemizing males and autistic people.

Feminist philosopher of neuroscience Cordelia Fine coined
the term "neurosexism" for theories like Baron-Cohen's that posit
male or female brains. On Fine's account, evidence reveals that,
neurologically, men and women are more alike than they are different. In her 2010 book, *Delusions of Gender: How Our Minds,
Society, and Neurosexism Create Difference*, Fine catalogues the
methodological flaws that she claims are endemic to brain sex
research. Further, she argues that the popular scientific accounts
of gendered brain differences are motivated not by the evidence but
by a popular desire for a biological basis for gender roles. Fine is
the most prominent member of a burgeoning new scholarly community of "neurofeminists"—feminist psychologists, philosophers,
and neuroscientists bent on debunking what they regard as methodological errors in brain sex theory.

9.4.3. Firestone on biodeterminism and technology: A radical proposal

Not all feminists object to the hypothesis that modern gender roles
are the products of our evolutionary history. Shulamith Firestone
(1945–2012) was a radical Marxist-feminist scholar who held biological imperatives are at the heart of human gender roles. Indeed,
in her *Dialectic of Sex*, Firestone argues that sexual dimorphism,
and the biological necessity of distinct human gender roles, is at

the heart of all other human class and caste systems. According to Firestone, the sorting that we do based on sex is the paradigm for all of the ways in which we sort and rank human beings. For Firestone, not only gender roles but all class-based oppression and injustice are explicable in terms of our biological character. However, for Firestone, this is no reason to accept sexism or other forms of injustice. While our ancestors needed to confine women's lives in a number of ways in order to ensure the continued existence of the species, Firestone advocates the use of new reproductive technologies to remove the responsibility of child-bearing from women. Once women are no longer required to bear children, argues Firestone, they can freely develop their capacities to the same degree as men. This will ultimately lead to the end of gender roles and, indeed, the end of class and inequality.

9.4.4. Nature or nurture?

At bottom, the debate between Darwin, evolutionary psychologists, and brain sex theorists on the one hand, and social constructivists about gender on the other, comes down to a familiar dichotomy: nature or nurture? If the evolutionary psychologists and their friends are right, then gender differences are biological in origin. If the social constructivists are right, gender differences are the product of socialization. How should we resolve this dilemma? Arguably, we would be better to *dissolve* the dilemma by rejecting the dichotomy that produced it. We know that much about human behaviour is biological in character, and we know that much is socialized. Why should we have to choose? We have good evidence that, for every-thing from intelligence test scores to contracting cancer, human behaviour typically results from a complex interaction between biology and environment. Why should we expect that gender roles would be any different?

What makes the debates around the biological basis of gender especially complex, however, is that the science of sex and gender is itself influenced both by physical evidence and by gendered social norms. In the next chapter, we will consider the ways in which variations in gender norms from one historical period to another drive theory change in sex science.

9.5. Questions for reflection

- Hubbard criticized evolutionary theorists for the often-specu-
  lative character of their work. Is this fair? Are they any more
  guilty of this than historians or cosmologists? If speculation
  is methodologically necessary in a field, is there a way to do
  it that avoids too much contamination by social norms?
- What do you think of Firestone's technologically driven uto-
  pia? Is it possible? Is it desirable? Do you think it would have
  the consequences Firestone predicts? Why or why not?
- At the end of the day, should we think of biology as destiny?
  How far should we go in this kind of thinking? What varieties of human malleability (social, cultural, psychological, or
  moral) might lead us to resist the full weight of the biodeterminist thesis?

9.6. Works cited and recommended reading

Baron-Cohen, Simon. *The Essential Difference: Men, Women
    and the Extreme Male Brain*. New York: Basic, 2004.
Bluhm, Robyn, Ann Jaap Jacobson, and Heidi Lene Maibom, Eds.
    *Neurofeminism: Issues at the Intersection of Feminist Theory
    and Cognitive Science*. London: Palgrave-Macmillan, 2012.
Buss, David. "Psychological Sex Differences: Origins Through
    Sexual Selection." *American Psychologist* 50.3 (1995):
    164–68.
Darwin, Charles. *Descent of Man, and Selection in Relation to
    Sex*. Princeton, NJ: Princeton University Press, 1981.
Fine, Cordelia. *Delusions of Gender: How Our Minds, Society,
    and Neurosexism Create Difference*. New York: Norton,
    2010.
Firestone, Shulamith. *The Dialectic of Sex: The Case For
    Feminist Revolution*. New York: Morrow, 1970.
Hubbard, Ruth. "Have Only Men Evolved?" Reprinted in
    Hubbard, *The Politics of Women's Biology*. New Brunswick,
    NJ: Rutgers, 1990. 87–106.
Morgan, Elaine. *The Descent of Woman*. London: Souvenir Press,
    1972.

Pinker, Steven. *The Blank Slate: The Modern Denial of Human Nature*. New York: Penguin, 2002.

Richardson, Sarah. *Sex Itself: The Search for Male and Female in the Human Genome*. Chicago: University of Chicago Press, 2013.

Roughgarden, Joan. *Evolution's Rainbow: Diversity, Gender, and Sexuality in Nature and People*. Berkeley: University of California Press, 2004.

CHAPTER 10

The One-Sex Model

10.1. Seeing versus seeing-as

In Chapter 9, we examined several accounts claiming that biological sex differences explain gender roles. In this chapter, we examine the converse view. For historian of science Thomas Laqueur, the "facts" about biological sex are themselves the result of our sociocultural beliefs about gender.

At first, this view might seem implausible. Isn't our biological nature more fundamental than our socio-cultural character? After all, biology is stable across cultures, but human cultures vary widely.

While it is true that the brute facts of biology are stable—more or less—across cultures, Laqueur argues that scientists—including sex scientists—do not trade in brute facts, but in interpretations of brute facts. To understand what he means, it will be useful to consider the distinction in the philosophy of science between "seeing" and "seeing as." The best way to do that is first-hand, by engaging in some careful observation.

Take some time and look through the images below. Attend closely to each of them, and make careful note of the artistic choices the artists made when rendering the images. What details are included in the images? What details are left out? After you've examined the images on your own, read the discussion of them.

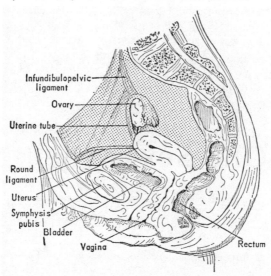

Figure 10.1: Female reproductive system, from C.H. Best and N.B. Taylor, *The Human Body: Its Anatomy and Physiology*, 4th ed. Copyright ©1963 by Brooks/Cole, a part of Cengage Learning, Inc. Reproduced with permission. www.cengage.com/permissions

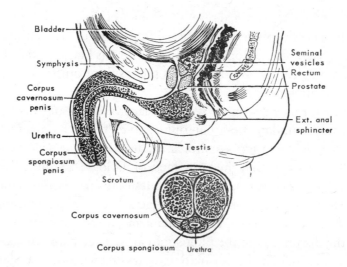

Figure 10.2: Male reproductive system, from C.H. Best and N.B. Taylor, *The Human Body: Its Anatomy and Physiology*, 4th ed. Copyright ©1963 by Brooks/Cole, a part of Cengage Learning, Inc. Reproduced with permission. www.cengage.com/permissions

What do you notice about these 1960s-era textbook illustrations of the female and male reproductive organs? At first they look pretty neutral, but on closer inspection there's nothing neutral about them. Even in these black and white drawings, you can discern the fair skin of a person of European origin. In places, it seems as if this skin is growing inside the person's body too, since you can see it despite the cross-section. It is perhaps worth noting too that both figures are comparatively slim. As well, the organs and tissues are healthy and youthful. The organs in the images are presented very neatly, all of them tidily arranged so that they are not blocking each other, and with no gore, or hair, or real-life messiness. As well, both illustrations include organs that are not strictly part of the reproductive system—the bladder, the rectum, and, for the male, the anal sphincter. (One wonders why the anal sphincter, while present in the female diagram, goes unlabelled.)

Notice that, among the features we have just noted, few are strictly necessary for anatomical illustration. That is, one could render anatomical illustrations of heavy-set people of colour, with hair on their bodies, and with messy organs, complete with blood and other tissue visible by cross-section. Such an illustration, however, would violate contemporary western conventions of anatomical illustration. Indeed, if the artist made any of those choices, you'd notice it right away. However, at first, you probably didn't notice many of the artistic choices in the illustrations above, because you've been trained over time to expect them.

The images incorporate artistic devices intended to make the relevant content salient to the reader. If you have ever performed dissections in science class, you'll notice how much easier it is to identify the organs in these images than it is to do so in the lab. In science class, it takes lots of practice to tell one organ from another, and to identify each organ. By contrast, these illustrations make sense the first time you see them. This is because the artist has designed them to be clear and accessible. The clean lines and shading make it easy to distinguish the organs from each other. However, it is worth observing that the price of this accessibility is a loss in accuracy. Many real-life details have been idealized away in order to make these diagrams easy to use.

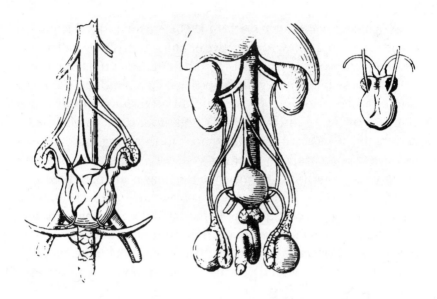

Figure 10.3: From Andreas Vesalius, *Tabulae Sex* (1538)

The third illustration, a sixteenth-century European anatomical illustration, is strikingly different from the first two in that there is no longer any effort to represent the reproductive organs in their abdominal context. What exactly are these organs anyway? They look unfamiliar. If you look at the lowermost centre of the figure on the left, you might see what looks like a penis. You might therefore assume that this is an illustration of the male reproductive system. But no, that penis-like organ is actually Vesalius's rendering of a vagina. To portray a vagina as penis-like in this way was typical of medical illustrations of the period. As Laqueur notes, on the Galenic medical model, the vagina was "imagined as an interior penis."[1] There's something else rather surprising about the drawing on the left—those two up-turned crescents growing from the topmost part of the vagina on either side of the uterus. This is Vesalius's representation of uterine horns. Again, under the Galenic model, women were believed to have horns growing out of their uteruses. (Some non-human mammals, like deer, actually have something called "uterine horns," but they're more like extended fallopian tubes than like horns.)

---

1   Thomas Laqueur, *Making Sex: Body and Gender from the Greeks to Freud*, 4.

For centuries, women's reproductive systems were represented in this way, with vaginas that resembled penises, ovaries that looked like internal testes, and with horns protruding from their uteruses. Of course, the anatomical illustrators of the day used cadavers as models, as do contemporary illustrators. How could they have looked at real human women's cadavers and seen penises and horns? To answer this question, once again recall your first experience dissecting an animal in science class. Remember how your teacher told you where to find all of the parts, and how hard it was actually to find them once you had a very real, and very messy, animal open in front of you? You had to be trained to find the organs, to recognize them, and to distinguish them from each other, didn't you? The organs didn't just offer themselves up to you in intelligible form as soon as you opened the incision you made, right? Well, just as you had to be trained to see the configuration of animal organs, so medical illustrators must be trained to see the configuration of human parts. In this way, they end up adopting conventions, seeing the organs as their teachers saw them, and sometimes reproducing the errors of those teachers.

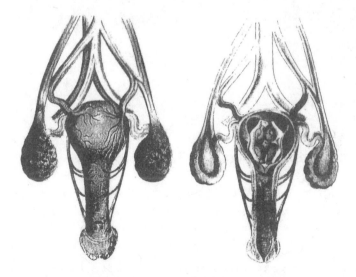

Figure 10.4: From Georg Bartisch, *Kunstbuche* (1575)

In this 1575 illustration by Georg Bartisch, we can see an especially obvious attempt to render the female reproductive system in a way that resembles the male. At first glance, in fact, this looks like a drawing of a penis and testicles. However, look at the cross-section on the right. See that little person just above the "penis"? That's a fetus, which means the thing just above the penis is a uterus, and the "penis" is in fact a vagina.

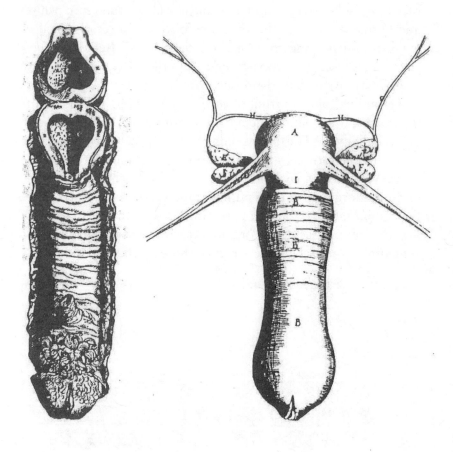

Figure 10.5: From Andreas Vesalius, *De humani corporis fabrica libri septem* (1543), and Vidus Vidius, *De anatome corporis humane* (1611)

Here we have two illustrations—the first a sixteenth-century illustration by Vesalius, and the second an early seventeenth-century illustration by Vidus Vidius—portraying very penile vaginas. The illustration on the right once again features very prominent uterine horns.

Figure 10.6A. Figures A-C from Yasukazu Minagaki (南小柿寧一),
Kaibo Zonshinzu anatomy scrolls (1819), Keio University Library

With this illustration, we shift from European drawings to Japanese ones. This illustration and the two that follow it are all taken from the Kaibo Zonshinzu anatomy scrolls by the nineteenth-century Japanese artist Yasukazu Minagaki. This time, the subject is clearly Asian, not European, and, judging from his wrinkles, is older than the people represented in the first two textbook illustrations. He has hair too, and, conspicuously, he has been decapitated. Observe the blood and rough tissue where his head was cut off and the trickle of blood coming from his mouth, which is held in a grimace. Unlike the putatively healthy abdomens of the first two images, this is clearly the head of a dead man. Indeed, most of Minagaki's subjects were criminals who had been decapitated as punishment for their crimes. Although he intended his illustrations for anatomical purposes—not shock value—he made no effort to conceal the features of his subjects, or the fact of their violent deaths.

Minagaki's next head also has hair, and also shows signs of suffering at the end of life. In particular, its mouth is open as if

Figure 10.6B

screaming. In this case, the skin has been removed from the head to reveal the muscle, cartilage, fat, and bone below. In this drawing as in the previous one, Minagaki has clearly just steadied the head on a surface and drawn it at the angle in which it appears to him. Thus, rather than the upright, front, or profile body part of the typical western anatomical illustration, we have here more naturalistic, less idealized angles.

In this final Minagaki illustration—a full torso—we again see evidence of decapitation, and again we see some of the distinctive

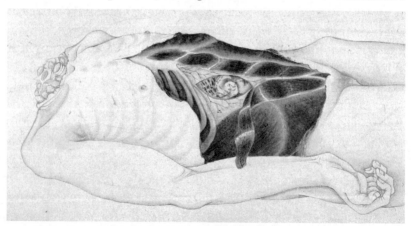

Figure 10.6C

features of the subject, in this case, a set of emaciated ribs. We can tell that the subject was poor. While Minagaki has omitted some details this time—genitalia and hair, for example—other aspects of the illustration are highly naturalistic. The body is supine in a very realistic pose, the right arm is clutched at its side, and the intestines spill out of the abdominal cavity.

This final illustration was created by American neurosurgeon Harvey Cushing in 1900. The skull is rendered with considerable attention to detail (richer detail, for instance, than that found in the first two images we looked at). However, the drawing, while detailed, is idealized. The angle of the skull is artful rather than

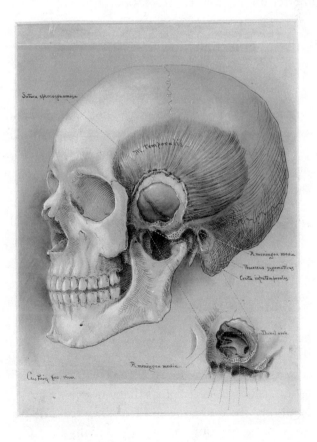

Figure 10.7: Harvey Cushing, "Showing relations of the middle meningeal artery to the operative foramen before and after elevation of the dura and exposure of the ganglion" (1900)

realistic, and evidence, both of the person's identity and of the context, has been removed. Moreover, we see that Cushing's real interest is not in the whole skull, but in the particular surgery being illustrated, and detailed in the inset. Again, in this drawing, as in all of the others we examined, we see evidence that the anatomical artist makes choices about what to represent and how to represent it. Some of these choices are conventional, as in the first few images; some are the result of the provenance of the models, as in the Minagaki illustrations; and some reflect the specialization of the artist, as in Cushing's drawing. All of these illustrations, in one way or another, differ from real bodies. Yet, all of them were used to better understand those real bodies.

The rise of objectivity in scientific illustration

In their ground-breaking study, "The Image of Objectivity," historians of science Lorraine Daston and Peter Galison trace the origin of objectivity as an ideal for illustrators of scientific atlases, and survey the different, sometimes competing, conceptions of objectivity that were at play for these illustrators. On Daston and Galison's account, the very notion of objectivity is itself always culturally inflected. The contemporary conception of objectivity, they argue, is a "conglomerate" of various earlier conceptions that do not always sit easily together. They write: "Modern objectivity mixes rather than integrates disparate components, which are historically and conceptually distinct. Each of these components has its own history, in addition to the collective history that explains how all of them came to be amalgamated into a single, if layered, concept."[2]

We noted earlier that working through medical illustrations such as these is a good way to come to understand the seeing versus seeing-as distinction. What exactly is this distinction? Philosophers use the term "seeing as" to express the way in which the character of our cognition—including the contextual factors and background assumptions that affect our cognition—actually shapes our perceptions of the world. One homely example is people's tendency to

2   Lorraine Daston and Peter Galison, "The Image of Objectivity," 82.

see faces in clouds and in the gnarled bark of trees. We see faces everywhere because one of the things we're "wired" to do is to interact with other people. It is to our evolutionary advantage to be able to identify faces *as* faces right away. However, this wiring means that sometimes we have false positives—again, a cloud or a bit of bark that, at first glance, reads to us as a face. We are seeing a cloud, but, for a second, we see it as a face. While this example is, as far as I know, universal across human cultures, lots of other instances of seeing-as are specific to particular cultures or subcultures, or even to specific people.

The concept of seeing-as originated with the great Austro-English philosopher, Ludwig Wittgenstein (1889–1951). In his *Philosophical Investigations* (1953), Wittgenstein uses the phrase to characterize those instances in which the same image can equally well be seen as two different things. His now-famous example was the "duckrabbit," which one might see as a duck in one moment and a rabbit in the very next moment. This *gestalt* switch makes us conscious of the role of interpretation in perception.

Figure 10.8: "Kaninchen und Ente" ("Rabbit and Duck"), *Fliegende Blätter*, (23 October 1892)

You can experience this first-hand by visiting a museum housing archaeological artifacts. If you examine the historical tools and other artifacts, you'll recognize some as hammers, pots, etc.

However, inevitably, you'll encounter one that you've never seen before and that you don't recognize. In this case, you won't see it as a specific *this* or *that*. You simply haven't been trained to do so. Instead, you'll have to content yourself with noticing its physical features and making some guesses about what it was for. You can't see it as anything (except perhaps as a mystery artifact) because you haven't been trained to do so.

The anatomical illustrations we examined highlight two classes of seeing-as—yours and the artists'. Most likely, you were at first unaware of the extent to which you've been trained to see the first few images as realistic and neutral, even though they are neither. By contrast, as you looked at the sixteenth- and seventeenth-century illustrations, you must have had moments of thinking "What the heck is that?" in the face of body parts you haven't been trained to see—in particular, uterine horns and penile vaginas. Looking at those images also put you face-to-face with the role of interpretation in the work of Vesalius and the other early modern anatomists. Due to their training and their culturo-historical context, when they saw various tissues and organs in female cadavers, they saw them as horns and inverted penises.

At bottom, Laqueur's provocative claim is that all scientific seeing is seeing-as. On Laqueur's view, scientists—including sex scientists like medical doctors and biologists—see the world as they've been enculturated to see it. Thus, any scientific view reflects the culture in which it is situated. On Laqueur's view, our cultural attitudes about gender actually partially construct our biological "facts" about sex. In the face of a confusing mass of tissue or a hard-to-parse physiological process, scientists unconsciously allow their cultural biases to creep into their interpretations.

This influence of culture on science is, on Laqueur's account, one of the main mechanisms behind scientific theory change. In particular, for our (and Laqueur's) purposes, it is the main mechanism behind the shift from the one-sex view to the two-sex view.

10.2. One sex or two?

Laqueur recounts the story of an innkeeper's daughter, comatose and presumed dead, and impregnated in this state by a visiting monk.

Laqueur compares two accounts of the story—a 1752 account by Antoine Louis and an 1836 account by Michael Ryan. Louis argued that the monk must have known that the young woman was alive because she must have given some "demonstrative signs"[3] of orgasm during intercourse. Eight decades later, Ryan disagreed, citing the case as evidence that a woman need not achieve orgasm in order to become pregnant. Laqueur attributes the disagreement between Louis and Ryan to the shift at the end of the eighteenth century from the one-sex view to the two-sex view. According to Laqueur, until this shift occurred, doctors and scientists, influenced by Aristotle and Galen, regarded females as (more or less) underdeveloped males.

Remember Aristotle's account in Chapter 3 of how sex differentiation occurs in the womb? Aristotle regarded the male and female reproductive systems as essentially the same system, with isomorphic parts. The main difference between the two systems, on his view, is that the male reproductive system functions better than the female. He thought that both males and females concoct reproductive fluid, but only males generate sufficient heat to concoct reproductive fluid well enough to contain the formal principle. Similarly, the female body is just the result of the father's less well-concocted semen failing to prevail over the mother's reproductive fluid. For Aristotle, therefore, females are essentially imperfectly made males, just as disabled offspring, or offspring who in other respects fail to resemble the father, are imperfectly made versions of a single ideal. Galen (129–c. 216), the great physician and medical scholar whose views dominated European medicine until the end of the sixteenth century, adopted a similar approach.

For Aristotle, the able-bodied male who resembles his father is the reproductive ideal. Offspring who fail to attain this ideal—for instance, due to lack of resemblance, disability, or femaleness—are all just misfires of varying degree. That is, they are not distinct types from able-bodied males; they are just poorer instances of the same type. It is in this sense that Laqueur regards Aristotle's view as a one-sex view.

On the Aristotelian/Galenic model, female reproductive organs are the same as male, only internal rather than external.

---

3   Laqueur, 2.

Since male orgasm is necessary for pregnancy, it was assumed that female orgasm was likewise necessary. It was for this reason that Louis insisted that the innkeeper's daughter must have appeared to the monk to be alive. Since she became pregnant, he reasoned, she must have had an orgasm, something the monk couldn't help but notice. By the end of the eighteenth century, however, doctors and biologists came to regard the male and female reproductive systems as heterogeneous; hence, Ryan's confidence that the innkeeper's daughter could conceive without orgasm.

> Laqueur says that under the Galenic model, women were regarded as having fleshly "desires [that] knew no bounds,"[4] but that this shifted around 1800 to the view that men enjoy sex more than women do—that men want sex and women want relationships. Can you think of artistic, literary, religious, or historical representations of men and women that align with this alleged shift? Can you think of any that do not align with the shift? Which, if either, of the two views do you think is prevalent today? Why?
>
> If Laqueur is right about his historical account, then for centuries many sexually unresponsive women who were not in fact having orgasms were understood by their partners—and themselves!—to be having orgasms. How could so many people have been so mistaken about this for so long?
>
> Historically, women impregnated by rape were often regarded as culpable for the pregnancy. How does thinking about the one-sex model help us to make sense of this practice, however misguided it was?

10.2.1. The rise of the two-sex model

By the nineteenth century, Laqueur tells us, the one-sex model gave way "to a new model of radical dimorphism, of biological divergence."[5] Laqueur identifies three main aspects of this shift:

---

4   Laqueur, 4.
5   Laqueur, 6.

1. Male and female bodies came to be regarded as radically heterogeneous.
2. Cell biologists came to regard cells—in particular anabolic and catabolic cells—as themselves gendered. The (female) anabolic cells were seen as slow, sluggish, and passive, and the (male) catabolic cells were seen as active, energetic, and even passionate! (Laqueur notes that the famous cell biologist, Patrick Geddes, attributed the difference between masculine and feminine gender roles to this deep, cellular difference between men and women.)
3. Biology—and in particular the sexed body—came to be regarded as the distinct, stable basis for cultural phenomena, rather than being enmeshed in those phenomena.

While Laqueur himself remains more or less agnostic on the first two aspects (even if he is somewhat skeptical about the second of them), he is definitely unconvinced by the third. To Laqueur, and contra the views of Enlightenment and post-Enlightenment thinkers, our biology and, in particular, our understanding of biology are just as embroiled in our culture as ever. We may tell ourselves that biology is stable and objective and culture is evanescent and subjective, but the latter continues to shape the former, and it is therefore difficult to maintain any view of biology that sees itself as insulated against the influences of cultural context.

What was the Enlightenment?

For Laqueur, the Enlightenment marks an important turning point in the history of the science of sex. The Enlightenment was a period in Western European thought spanning the 1650s to the 1780s. The period was characterized by revolutions in scientific, philosophical, religious, and political thought. In particular, Enlightenment thinkers emphasized the capacity of individual human beings to arrive at an understanding of the world by means of reason and science. This marked a huge shift from the previous centuries' emphasis on religious authority as the source of knowledge. For one of the fathers of the Enlightenment, French philosopher René Descartes, all that is required for knowledge is careful, sustained attention by individual thinkers, this attention sharpened by a bit of healthy skepticism. Prior to the Enlightenment, philosophy was considered the province of the well-educated few. With the Enlightenment, came the view that anyone, regardless of education, class, or gender, could do philosophy. Philosophical salons sprang up around Paris, with men and women from many different walks of life as participants. The twin Enlightenment ideas that human beings are essentially rational, and that all human beings have equal capacity for rational thought, were amazingly liberatory. Eventually, these ideas led to the two great revolutions of the eighteenth century, to new nation-states founded on democratic ideals, and to the abolition of slavery. We'll look more closely at Enlightenment thought in Chapter 11 when we discuss Rousseau and Wollstonecraft.

Our post-Enlightenment optimism about science might lead us to think that the shift from the one-sex model to the two-sex model is scientific progress from a false view to a true one. Laqueur, however, problematizes the notion of scientific progress, and along with it the idea that there are objectively true or false views. Laqueur points out that the scientific evidence lagged behind the changing attitudes toward the sexes. For instance, "the re-evaluation of pleasure occurred more than a century before reproductive physiology could come to its support with any kind of deserved authority."[6] If scientific evidence didn't prompt the new approach to sexual biology, then what did? Laqueur attributes the shift to two distinct historical developments, one epistemological, one political.

Epistemologically, the Enlightenment saw a new approach to the world in which it was no longer taken for granted (as it had been in the Aristotelian tradition) that all parts of the universe fit together neatly, each with its own particular role and place. This cleared a space for the concept of sexual dimorphism. Politically, the rise of equality as an ideal threw into question the very idea that women were necessarily inferior to men. As the revolutions of the eighteenth century overthrew political hierarchies with cries

---

6   Laqueur, 9.

of "Liberty! Equality! Fraternity!" biological hierarchies too became untenable.

Thus, while some biodeterminists suggest that sexual dimorphism entails female subordination, Laqueur on the contrary sees the notion of equality of the sexes as at the very foundation of the idea of sexual dimorphism. In Chapter 11, we will examine two Enlightenment-era views about the comparative virtues of the sexes.

10.3. Questions for reflection

- Think back to our Chapter 1 discussion of Kessler and McKenna and their concept of gender attribution. In what sense is gender attribution understandable as a variety of seeing-as? Are any of the other gender concepts Kessler and McKenna delineate similarly expressible as types of seeing-as?
- Laqueur adduces evidence that doctors and scientists first ignored the differences between males and females, then exaggerated them. Do you think this happens in contemporary science? Can you think of any examples in which recent/current views in a scientific domain have undergone a similar shift?
- Laqueur is skeptical of the notion of scientific progress. For him, science is constituted by culture and necessarily reflects that culture. Do you agree? Why or why not?

10.4. Works cited and recommended reading

Daston, Lorraine and Peter Galison. "The Image of Objectivity." *Representations* 40 (Fall 1992): 81–128.

Laqueur, Thomas. *Making Sex: Body and Gender from the Greeks to Freud*. Cambridge, MA: Harvard University Press, 1990.

Wittgenstein, Ludwig. *Philosophical Investigations*. 4th ed. Ed. and trans. P.M.S. Hacker and Joachim Schulte. Oxford: Wiley-Blackwell, 2009.

CHAPTER 11

Difference and Equality

11.1. Two Enlightenment thinkers

In Chapter 10, we looked at Thomas Laqueur's argument that egalitarian thinking lies at the heart of the "two-sex model." Unlike the putative "one-sex model," which treats femaleness as a kind of deficit, the two-sex model allows for females to be very different from males without being worse than them. In this chapter, we will look at two examples of the kind of egalitarian thinking that Laqueur identifies with the eighteenth century.

Swiss philosopher Jean-Jacques Rousseau (1712–78) was one of the great inspirations for the French Revolution. While Rousseau was a champion of egalitarianism, he argued that women ought to be subordinate to men. Interestingly, though, as we'll see, this political inegalitarianism was grounded in a two-sex model that seems to treat men and women as different but equal.

Rousseau's remarks on the education of women were one of the motive forces behind English philosopher Mary Wollstonecraft's (1759–97) *A Vindication of the Rights of Woman*. While Wollstonecraft stops short of arguing that women are equal to men, she cautions that there is no evidence that they are necessarily inferior to men.

If they are inferior, she writes, it is because we have trained them to be so. Only once women have received the same education as men will we be able to judge whether they really are equal.

11.2. Rousseau on the education of girls

Rousseau was, among other things, a philosopher of education, and one of the early influences behind what nowadays gets called "child-centred education." On his view, education should focus on the development of moral traits, not the memorization of facts and figures. His main elaboration of his philosophy of education occurs in *Emilius and Sophia; Or, A New System of Education* (1762). He devotes four books of that volume to the question of how to educate boys (personified as Emile), and the fifth to the education of girls (personified as Sophia).

Rousseau starts his discussion of the education of girls by claiming that "in every thing, which does not regard the sex, woman is the same as man," but that in things relating to sex, women are radically different from men.[1] The trick, he says, is figuring which human features relate to sex, and hence admit of this heterogeneity, and which do not relate to sex, and therefore do not admit of heterogeneity.

He suggests as a heuristic that when we see similarities between men and women, we judge them to be traits of the species, and that when we perceive differences, we judge them to be sex traits. Notice that this method is biodeterministic. It assumes that all differences between men and women are natural differences, rather than socialized ones. (See Chapter 9 for a refresher on biodeterminism.)

Rousseau continues that, not only are male and female sex traits very different from each other, but that there is no comparison between them. In essence, you should no more judge a female trait by male standards than you should judge cats by the standards used in dog shows.

According to Rousseau, the different characteristics of the sexes are visible in the sex act itself, wherein, he reports, men are "active

---

1   Jean-Jacques Rousseau, *Emilius and Sophia: Or, A New System of Education*, 2.

and strong," possessing "power and will," while women are "passive and weak" and make "little resistance." Men are sexually pleasing because they are strong, says Rousseau. It is the woman's role to inflame a man's desires by resisting him just enough that he must deploy his strength to prevail over her. However, this poses little obstacle, since women's sexual attractiveness resides in their weakness.

No means no?

Nowadays, we are regularly urged that in matters of sexual consent no means no, and further that only yes means yes. If a prospective sexual partner resists, one should neither force nor seek to persuade her to take part in the sex act. Rousseau's view that men not only do force their partners, but ought to do so is in stark contrast to this approach. However, it bears observing that this understanding of sexual consent is comparatively new. Until recently in many cultures, it was expected that "good girls" would make a show of resisting men's sexual advances, all the while expecting the men to redouble their efforts when rebuffed in this way. Indeed, lots of romance fiction still employs this device. Moreover, some feminist theorists, such as Andrea Dworkin, have argued that heterosexual sex fundamentally involves the coercion of women. So, is Rousseau just being honest about what sex is really like, or is he an unwitting date-rape apologist?

In an observation that anticipates Beauvoir (Chapter 4) and Firestone (Chapter 9), but which lacks the spirit of critique that animates both of those authors, Rousseau notes that, in virtue of their reproductive role, women feel the consequences of their sex most of the time while men only feel their maleness from time to time. The continued survival of the family and indeed of the species, argues Rousseau, depends upon women not only bearing and raising children, but knitting their families together with their womanly patience, tenderness, and spotless virtue. In order to be willing to support his children, a man must be convinced that they are indeed *his* children, Rousseau tells us. Thus, women must not only remain faithful to their husbands; they must appear so virtuous that their husbands can have no doubt of their fidelity. Thus, for Rousseau, the overall well-being of society depends on the woman's function of persuading the man to marry her, and to remain with her to support his children.

Consequently, his prescriptions for the education of women are primarily intended to train girls to acquire the kinds of virtues that will allow them to attract and keep husbands. According to Rousseau, such education not only benefits the family and the broader society, it also benefits women themselves. While men are capable of ensuring their own survival, women lack the ability to support themselves and must therefore attach themselves to men who will provide for them. Now, no man has any reason to take on a dependent if there is no benefit to him. Thus, if women wish to ensure their own survival, they must make themselves sufficiently pleasing to men that the men will be willing to support them. It is by cultivating their beauty, by listening to men talk and laughing at their jokes, and creating a loving home that women earn their keep. It is therefore highly in their interest to be educated in order to perform such tasks well. Rousseau urges that women have sufficient good sense to recognize that serving men well is in their interest, and that those educating girls (in particular, their mothers) should explain this motive to them.

Rousseau further maintains that girls ought to be subject to restraint from a very young age since women must live their lives in a condition of restraint. Accustoming little girls to restraint early on therefore helps them to get used to their lifelong condition, with the result that this condition becomes less irksome for them in adulthood.

Since women's main duties, unlike men's, are to charm men, to persuade others of their fidelity, and to manage the household, Rousseau prescribes very different forms of education for boys and girls. We must, for instance, cultivate the amusing "prattle" of girls, but with it their awareness of their words' impressions on others. When boys talk, he advises, we should ask them what point they are trying to make. When girls talk, we should ask them what people will think of their remarks. Similarly, while boys should be trained to express their ideas, girls should be trained to become accustomed to being interrupted.

Likewise, Rousseau argues that boys should be trained in moral reasoning whereas girls should be taught to obey authority on matters of morality and religion. Similarly, boys should be trained in abstract and speculative reasoning, while girls are trained to focus on the practical.

While Rousseau's prescriptions for the education of girls seem to treat females as inferior to males, Rousseau denies that this is his view. Women are only inferior to men, he writes, when judged by the male standard. Males and females have different virtues, he argues. Males should be judged according to the male standard, and females according to the female. The two sets of virtues complement each other and lead to social accord, on his view. Males and females, he suggests, are different but equal.

Feminist essentialism?

One variety of feminism that emerged toward the end of the twentieth century is feminist essentialism. Feminist essentialists maintain that there really are essential differences between men and women. They argue that womanly traits are insufficiently valued due to society's bias in favour of men. They urge feminists to cultivate and celebrate these womanly virtues and to work to increase the esteem in which they are held in society. Two figures working in this broad tradition are Carol Gilligan, who argues from a psychological perspective that women are naturally more nurturing and other-focused than men, and Luce Irigaray (whom we discussed in Chapter 4), who argues that women both perceive the world differently and communicate differently than men do. Do you think Rousseau was an early feminist essentialist? Why or why not?

From a present-day perspective, it is difficult to see the social roles that Rousseau ascribes to women and men, and the educational imperatives he associates with them, in the way that Rousseau himself did. Whereas he thought of these roles and imperatives as growing out of natural differences between the sexes, our own historical hindsight leads us to suspect that his view of those differences amounts to little more than a mirroring of the socially prevalent gender assumptions of his time and place. However, when we bear in mind the likelihood that eighteenth-century conceptions of the sexes bore this kind of socio-cultural imprint, we can perhaps arrive at deeper understanding of Rousseau's claims on behalf of sexual equality.

If, to our eyes, Rousseau's women look inferior to Rousseau's men, it is arguably because we no longer accept the inevitability of the specific gender roles he assigns to the sexes. However, from a point of view like Rousseau's that accepts these roles and requirements as inevitable, it would make little sense to evaluate one sex according to standards appropriate to the other, or to devise educational programmes that didn't take stock of the (allegedly) natural differences between the sexes. Moreover, it is far from obvious that the requirements of virtuous womanhood were in any way less exacting or onerous than those of virtuous manhood even in Rousseau's time. For Rousseau, it makes sense to ask how women can become better women, or men better men, but there is no reasonable way to pose the question of whether men are better than women.

11.3. Wollstonecraft: God, rationality, and equality

Mary Wollstonecraft's reply to Rousseau is, at bottom, a theological one. If women have souls, she argues, then they must be held to the same standard of virtue (that is, the same moral standard) as men are—God's standard. On Wollstonecraft's account, God endowed us with the capacity for rational thought precisely so that we could judge rightly in moral matters. It must be possible for us—women included—to be virtuous; otherwise, God's creation would have been flawed. While Wollstonecraft admits that women display follies, caprices, and vices, she attributes this to their lack of a proper education: "Behold ... the natural effect of ignorance!"[2]

Rousseau had argued that while male virtue and female virtue comprise distinct and separable moral standards, women must nevertheless turn to men for rational guidance in morality, just as children turn to their parents. In reply, Wollstonecraft argues that

---

2   Mary Wollstonecraft, *A Vindication of the Rights of Men and a Vindication of the Rights of Woman*, 87.

if women are childlike, it is because men have systematically infantilized them. To reduce adult persons to childish ways in order to
better govern them Wollstonecraft condemns as unphilosophical.
Contrary to the received view in her time, Wollstonecraft argues
that women ought not to be innocent. "Innocent," she tells us, is an
acceptable term for children; not so for men or women. For them,
it is just the polite term used to characterize weakness.

Revolutionaries and counter-revolutionaries

While Wollstonecraft opposed Rousseau's views on the nature and
education of women, in another great eighteenth-century battle,
they were allies. The politically progressive Rousseau was one of
the major influences on the French Revolution. "Man is born free,
and yet we see him everywhere in chains,"[3] Rousseau famously
wrote. When the French peasantry sought to escape those chains
through revolution, Edmund Burke, the great Irish statesman and
philosopher, publicly condemned the revolutionaries. In his remarks,
he singled out Rousseau in particular for blame. The revolutionaries, argued Burke, took Rousseau as their inspiration; the result, he
claimed, was an unnatural and dangerous new morality, untethered
from virtue. Wollstonecraft wrote her *A Vindication of the Rights of
Men* (1790) as an explicit reply to Burke. There, she condemned
the aristocracy and argued persuasively for the natural equality of
human beings. This volume both brought Wollstonecraft to fame
and inspired her follow-up book, *A Vindication of the Rights of
Woman*. Thus, it was in indirectly allying herself with Rousseau
and his ideological descendants that Wollstonecraft established her
intellectual reputation and her distinctive feminist voice.

Wollstonecraft proceeds from her Christian starting-point to
argue that the best education, for man or woman, should have the
aim of "co-operat[ing] ... with the supreme Being."[4] To this end, it
must "strengthen the body and form the heart."[5] Virtuous beings

3   Jean-Jacques Rousseau, *An Inquiry into the Nature of the Social Contract;
     or Principles of Political Right*, 3.
4   Wollstonecraft, 89.
5   Wollstonecraft, 89.

are virtuous because of their capacity for reason, she continues. Women have been drawn out of this rational realm, their natural realm, by "false refinement."[6] All of the writers on women's education to date, she charges, have contributed to this false refinement and to making women weak and less rational.

Family resemblance?

Mary Wollstonecraft was not the only woman in her family to be influenced by Rousseau. Her daughter, Mary Shelley, was a great admirer of Rousseau. Indeed, many scholars argue that she based the monster in her novel *Frankenstein* (1818) on Rousseau's "natural man." If so, then it seems likely that Shelley, like her mother, didn't take Rousseau's views to be above criticism.

Wollstonecraft was, in many respects, a typical eighteenth-century philosopher. Like the most famous and important philosopher of that period, Immanuel Kant, she regarded human beings' capacity for rational thought as separate from and nobler than their capacity for sense perception or emotional responses. Like Kant, Wollstonecraft saw our senses and emotions as tugging us away from rationality and hence from virtue. She regarded the education of girls as especially problematic since it was intentionally geared toward cultivating girls' senses and emotions, unlike boys' education, which sought to cultivate their rationality. This, she argued, made it more difficult for women than for men to make moral judgments and to strive to attain to godlike virtue.

Wollstonecraft admits that if men attain perfection of moral judgment in adulthood, it might make sense for a wife to cling to her husband's understanding as "the graceful ivy, clasping the oak that supported it, would form a whole in which strength and beauty would be equally conspicuous."[7] However, she maintains, many men are themselves like overgrown children and hence ill-suited to this role.

---

6   Wollstonecraft, 90.
7   Wollstonecraft, 90.

One of the biggest obstacles to women's rationality, according to Wollstonecraft, is that girls are not educated in an orderly way, and moreover, they are raised to disregard order. While boys are taught first principles and theoretical foundations of various disciplines, girls' education is desultory—unfocused and erratic. To illustrate this, she employs an analogy between women and soldiers. Like women, she claims, soldiers are sent into the world without first receiving a full education on theoretical matters. They too acquire superficial knowledge through happenstance rather than systemic knowledge by design. The result: soldiers, like women, are vain and superficial, and blindly obedient to authority. Wollstonecraft regards this as evidence that it was the particular manner in which women are educated and not their biological sex that makes them fickle and short-sighted. When men are educated in the same way, she tells us, we see the same results.

Why would men seek to limit women's intellectual potential? On Wollstonecraft's account, tyrants and sensualists both try to keep women in the dark—tyrants because they want power and sensualists because they want sexual playthings. Educated women would not be so easily controlled by either type of man; it is ignorance and lack of intellectual development that leads to the unquestioning obedience that women display towards men.

Wollstonecraft several times openly admits that, even once educated in the same manner as men, women might turn out to be inferior to men. Still, she argues, if they have souls and were made in God's image, then the same standard of virtue holds for them as for men. They just won't be as good at attaining to the ideal within that standard. After all, she asks, how could the virtues be different for men and women if God provides virtue's one eternal standard?

Towards the end of her discussion, Wollstonecraft moves on from discussing education to discussing marriage. Love, she claims, is no basis for a marriage. Love is a passing emotion; only true friendship lasts. If women are all their lives socialized to seek the love of a man, then when the husband's love for his wife fades, as is natural, with time, the wife will seek love from another man. Love is evanescent; its passing leads to jealousy. Marriage should be based on deep and abiding friendship between equals.

11.3.1. A long journey

The cases of Rousseau and Wollstonecraft are evidence that equality doesn't happen all at once. Rousseau argued for the equality of all men, but regarded women as subordinate. Wollstonecraft argued for women's equality with men, but had harsh words for Muslims and the Chinese. Moreover, her advice to women to eschew the primping and charming behaviour that was then deemed necessary to get a husband was advice that, arguably, would have been impossible for many poor women to take. Finally, of course, it would have been impossible for eighteenth-century thinkers like Rousseau or Wollstonecraft to think about equality for LGBTQ people. A pessimist might say that even the champions of equality often cannot see beyond their own wheelhouse. However, a more optimistic response is to think of the quest for equality among human beings as a long journey, in which each small step puts us further ahead.

Ultimately, the Rousseau-Wollstonecraft debate brings into sharper focus the contrast between those who, like Darwin and some evolutionary psychologists (Chapter 9), regard gender differences as ultimately explicable by biological facts, and those who, like Beauvoir and Freud (Chapter 4) and Money (Chapters 7 and 8), take a developmental approach. Another way to express the question at issue is as follows: "Are sex or gender socially constructed?" In the next and final chapter, we'll try to make sense of that question. What do you think? Are you an optimist or a pessimist about equality? Why?

11.4. Questions for reflection

- Rousseau argues that it is women, not men, who are to blame for educating girls to be vain and coquettish since it is primarily women and not men who educate girls. Do you agree? Why or why not?
- Do you think that it was, in Rousseau's time, genuinely in the interest of girls to be educated in the way he proposes? What about today?

- What do you think? Are moral decisions merely rational decisions, as Wollstonecraft thought, or do they have sensual or emotional aspects too?
- Wollstonecraft's argument in favour of a single standard for men and women is grounded in the theological notion that God created men and women in his own image. Can you think of a way to tweak her argument so that it would have force for members of non-Judeo-Christian religions, or for atheists? Why or why not?

11.5. Works cited and recommended reading

Dworkin, Andrea. *Intercourse*. New York: Free Press, 1987.

Gilligan, Carol. *In a Different Voice: Psychological Theory and Women's Development*. Cambridge, MA: Harvard University Press, 1993.

Rousseau, Jean-Jacques. *Emilius and Sophia: Or, A New System of Education*. 2nd ed. Vol. 4. London: Becket and Hondt, 1763.

——. *An Inquiry into the Nature of the Social Contract; or Principles of Political Right*. Dublin: Jones, 1791.

Shelley, Mary. *Frankenstein; or, The Modern Prometheus*. Ed. Susan J. Wolfson. New York: Pearson Longman, 2007.

Wollstonecraft, Mary. *A Vindication of the Rights of Men and a Vindication of the Rights of Woman*. Cambridge: Cambridge University Press, 1995.

CHAPTER 12

Sex/Gender
as Social Construction

12.1. Our story so far

While sex and gender have occupied the forefront of our attention in this volume, the notion of social construction has throughout lurked in the background.

Borges's strange and unsettling encyclopedia excerpt (Chapter 1) hinted that our usual taxonomies might themselves be arbitrary. Foucault's three serious doubts (Chapter 2) seemed to suggest that both sexual repression and the very *idea* of sexual repression are the outgrowths of underlying systems of power. In the same chapter, Kessler and McKenna problematized the apparent inevitability and simplicity of the gender binary. Chapter 3's visit to the Garden of Eden revealed the historical contingency of Judeo-Christian thought. In the next chapter, Beauvoir raised the radical proposal that woman is a social construct—made rather than born—while Irigaray sketched an alternative vision of humanity informed by the female rather than the male imaginary. Chapters 5 through 8 made the two-sex/two-gender account seem anything but inevitable, while Chapter 9 surveyed some biodeterministic rejoinders to social constructivists about gender. In Chapter 10, Thomas Laqueur attributed the scientific shift from the one-sex model to the two-sex model to social rather than evidential factors. In Chapter 11, Wollstonecraft responded to Rousseau that society, not nature, made women weaker than men.

In one way or another then, every chapter in this volume has entertained the social constructivist hypothesis. So, what exactly is it to be socially constructed, and what does it have to do with sex and gender?

Put simply, a thing or idea is socially constructed if it is the product of human society rather than being naturally occurring. However, this definition only goes part-way to explaining social constructivism. After all, a great many things in our lives are the products of human society, but we do not bother to claim of all, or even most of them, that they are socially constructed. If we don't care that cars are socially constructed, then why should we care whether or not sex or gender are?

In this chapter, we will seek to better understand exactly what social constructivism is. First, we'll consider Ian Hacking's attempt to disambiguate between different kinds of social construction claims. Then, with a better understanding of social constructivism in hand, we'll examine Susan Bordo's provocative argument for the view that not just female gender roles but female bodies themselves are socially constructed.

12.2. Hacking: The social construction of what?

One of the most useful guides to thinking about social construction is *The Social Construction of What?* by Canadian philosopher of science, Ian Hacking. This book is Hacking's response to the so-called science wars that raged in the 1990s. The science wars were a series of debates between scientific realists (philosophers and scientists who regard scientific claims as more or less objective representations of reality) and post-modernist critics, who argued that scientific "facts" are socially constructed. (Thomas Laqueur's argument, which we looked at in Chapter 10, is a nice example of such a social construction account of human sexual biology.) At their most polemical, the science wars sometimes looked like a bunch of people on one side of the debate arguing that nothing is socially constructed and a bunch of people on the other side claiming that everything is.

Hacking waded into this business in typical Canadian peacekeeping style and urged that the truth lay somewhere in between and that, in order to arrive at a sensible position, it was first necessary to think more clearly about the very notion of social construction.

Hacking begins his introduction to the volume by providing an A to Z (but excluding X, which he reserves for use as a variable) list of various things that, according to recent book titles at the time he was writing, are said to be socially constructed. The list covers a wide range of types of things—authorship, the child viewer of television, facts, gender, quarks, and women refugees. "What a lot of things are said to be socially constructed!" observes Hacking.[1]

A great fear of relativism

The concept of relativism is closely related to that of social construction. A social constructivist about X believes that X, rather than being inevitable, is the contingent product of its social milieu (or of an earlier one). By contrast, a relativist about X claims that there is no objective truth about X—that there are, at best, a plurality of contextual truths that hold only relative to particular socio-cultural standpoints. For instance, a relativist about morality would say that there is no objective moral standard, but that there are a variety of differing moralities, the standards of which are valid only within the particular communities or cultures that acknowledge them. Hacking attributes much of the anxiety that often surrounds social construction claims to "a great fear of relativism."[2] He attributes to some "intellectuals and nationalists" the worry that "relativism entail(s) that any kind of religious fundamentalism is as good as any kind of science."[3]

While Hacking's primary interest is in the science wars, he observes that "talk of social construction has become common coin,

---

1   Ian Hacking, *The Social Construction of What?*, 1.
2   Hacking, 4.
3   Hacking, 5.

valuable for political activists and familiar to anyone who comes across current debates about race, gender, culture, or science."[4] This is unsurprising, he notes, since there is something deeply liberating about social construction claims. To claim that something—whether it be authorship or women refugees—is socially constructed is to say that the *status quo* with respect to that thing is not inevitable. It could change if the right social and historical conditions come into being. He cautions, however, that social construction analyses are not always liberating in this way.

Claiming, for instance, that anorexia nervosa is socially constructed arguably does little to help the girls and women (and sometimes boys and men) suffering and dying from it. "Social construction theses are liberating," he wryly observes, "chiefly for those who are on the way to being liberated."[5]

Hacking urges the importance of understanding what social constructivists are actually saying. On his view, however, the way to do this is not to define "social construction." Instead, he argues that we should attend to what social constructivists are trying to accomplish with their social construction theses. "Don't ask for the meaning," he advises, "ask what's the point."[6] One way to understand Hacking's approach is to think of it as a pragmatic one rather than an epistemological one. He is concerned with the uses to which claims are put, not solely with the truth of those claims. Thus, his approach is in some respects similar to Foucault's. (For a reminder about Foucault's approach, see Chapter 2.)

12.2.1. Grades of commitment

While the types of items in Hacking's list of things said to have been socially constructed vary widely, Hacking observes that what unites many of the corresponding social construction claims is an underlying consciousness-raising aim. In general, he observes, social construction claims both deny the inevitability of and critique the *status quo*. This critique can be modest or radical.

---

4   Hacking, 2.
5   Hacking, 2.
6   Hacking, 5.

Consider critiques of gender roles, for instance. First, it would be rather futile to critique gender roles if we didn't think we could do anything about them. So, the very fact of critique already implies the possibility, or at least the hope, of change. Second, two people who agree that we might be able to change gender roles and that they ought to be changed might nonetheless disagree on just how much change is required. A feminist essentialist might argue that the roles themselves are generally fine, but that we should attach greater prestige to traditionally feminine gender roles like childcare and eldercare. By contrast, a radical feminist might argue that gender roles are so bad that we ought to abolish them and rebuild our social structures without them. Both of these approaches amount to critique. Where they differ is in what Hacking terms "grades of commitment."

Hacking identifies three main grades of commitment that may be associated with social construction claims about any X:

1. X need not have existed, or need not be at all as it is. X, or X as it is at present, is not determined by the nature of things; it is not inevitable.
2. X is quite bad as it is.
3. We would be much better off if X were done away with, or at least radically transformed.[7]

On this scheme, the feminist essentialist's claim probably belongs somewhere between 1 and 2, while the radical feminist's claim aligns with 3. They are both social construction claims about gender roles; as such, they both accept that gender roles might be otherwise. But as claims they show different grades of commitment.

While claims of the first degree ("X need not have existed") seem quite modest, Hacking points out that in some sense the thesis that X need not have existed is the most radical of the three since it sets the stage for all further social construction talk about X. Moreover, one only claims that X need not have existed if it is not at first obvious. No one would ever bother to point out that Ikea or the Olympics need not have existed because it's obvious that they

---

7   Hacking, 6.

are sociocultural products. Of course, Ikeas aren't inevitable! We only bother to point out the social-constructedness of things when some people take them to be inevitable.

This insight leads Hacking to formulate the following background claim that, he tells us, serves as the historical precondition for statements (1)–(3):

> 0. In the present state of affairs, X is taken for granted; X appears to be inevitable.[8]

Put differently, we only ever bother to claim that something is socially constructed when in some prior time it was taken to be the natural way of things.

And, as our above placement of the feminist essentialist claim revealed, there are more than three grades of commitment. Hacking sketches three, but his approach admits of finer-grained applications.

12.2.2. Objects of social construction claims

Of course, social construction claims vary not only in their degree of commitment but also in what sort of thing they claim to be socially constructed—the thing that is represented by "X" in the formulations above. While Hacking warns that the division between the kinds of things said to be socially constructed can get complicated, he offers three rough-and-ready categories: *objects*, *ideas*, and *elevator words*.

Objects, for Hacking, are items in the world, whether material, like rocks, or immaterial, like gender relations. By "ideas" he means "conceptions, beliefs, attitudes, theories," whether private or public. He also counts as ideas groupings, classifications, and kinds, but not the things that are included within those classifications. Thus, while "woman" names an idea, "this woman, Marjane" names an object. Similarly, while "woman refugee" names an idea, any particular group of woman refugees counts as an object.

Finally, Hacking uses the term "elevator words" to pick out such high level, abstract terms as "facts," "truth," "reality," and

---

8   Hacking, 12.

"knowledge." He wryly calls them elevator words because, once introduced, they quickly change the level of discourse. Put simply, the conversation takes a huge turn when interlocutors move from discussing, say, women and men to discussing truth and reality. Most of the social construction claims we have looked at in this volume are claims about objects or ideas, not about "elevator words." Indeed, most of the social construction claims anyone makes are claims about objects or ideas. Nonetheless, Hacking includes the category of "elevator words" because, from time to time, someone claims that truth itself or reality itself is socially constructed. Indeed, it is social construction claims about "elevator words" (or rather, about the things they represent) that arguably give all social construction claims a bad name in certain parts of academe.

Hacking's motives for elaborating the two divisions that he does—that is, the grades-of-commitment division and the objects-of-social-construction claims division—is to make clear that all social construction claims are not created equal. Two social construction claims may share an object but may differ with respect to grade of commitment. Conversely, two similarly radical claims might be about very different objects.

The matrix

Hacking makes clear in his discussion that he is especially interested in ideas. This should not be a surprise. Social construction claims about ideas are more important and more liberatory than those about objects, and more plausible than those about elevator words.

Moreover, as Hacking is keen to point out, ideas both affect and are affected by the social contexts in which they occur. Hacking describes the social context inhabited by ideas as a *matrix*. On Hacking's account, arguments that some idea, X, is socially constructed are typically less motivated by an interest in the origin of X than by concern for X's role within the matrix of institutions, texts, legal and political entities, and material infrastructure it inhabits.

Ideas within their matrices matter to people at least in part by affecting how those people feel about themselves, and by thereby affecting the kinds of people that they are. Classifications and the matrices in which they are embedded affect people's attitudes and actions. If you classify someone as a single mother, she will be aware of the classification. It will affect how she perceives herself, which social programs she utilizes, with whom she socializes, and more. Moreover, as these facts about individual single mothers gradually change as a consequence of the classification, the classification itself changes. People are, as a result of their classifications, socially constructed as certain kinds of people, and as they are, the classifications must be adjusted to reflect the new reality. Hacking refers to this feedback loop of classifications and individuals in the matrix as the "looping effect of human kinds."

12.3. Constructing the body

In her "The Body and the Reproduction of Femininity," feminist theorist Susan Bordo analyzes three classes of just this kind of interaction—three ways in which women's conscious or unconscious awareness of the ideas associated with the classification "woman" actually constructs them as individuals of a certain type. What is striking about Bordo's account is that it is not merely the women's behaviour or beliefs that are affected by their classification but their bodies.

She makes this explicit in the very first paragraph where she provocatively writes

> The body—what we eat, how we dress, the daily rituals through which we attend to the body—is a medium of culture, ... a surface on which the central rules, hierarchies, and even metaphysical commitments of a culture are inscribed and thus reinforced through the concrete language of the body.[9]

Bordo agrees with French philosopher Pierre Bourdieu that culture is continuously, in a variety of practical ways, changing our very bodies

---

9   Susan Bordo, "The Body and the Reproduction of Femininity: A Feminist Appropriation of Foucault," 13.

One need only compare photos of people from different eras to see what Bordo and Bourdieu have in mind. The great Hollywood stars of the 1930s looked very different from today's celebrities. Whereas old-style leading men like Cary Grant and Jimmy Stewart were gangly and lean, today's leading men are sculpted and muscular.

Conversely, the curvy leading ladies opposite Grant and Stewart have been replaced by size 0 waifs. In a recent film, *The Devil Wears Prada*, the protagonist is berated for wearing size 6 clothing. Why, in less than a century, has there been such a shift in the ideals of beauty for leading men and women? It's not because the species has physically changed. Rather, various subtle and not-so-subtle cultural shifts have led men and women to exercise different regimens on their bodies than they used to. The result: changes in culture have produced changes in bodies.

This should come as no surprise. We change our bodies in response to cultural demands all the time. Take a moment to think about the intentional changes you've made to your body in the past six months. What have you shaved? Waxed? Trimmed? Plumped? Pumped? Do you go to the gym? To Weight Watchers? To the hairdresser? To the tattoo artist? You probably changed something about your body today.

Bordo argues that these culturally contingent regimens render our bodies (to use Foucault's term) *docile*. We are accustomed to the habituation, regulation, and regimentation of our bodies. We don't fight it. On Bordo's account, these docile bodies can undermine our conscious values. We consciously believe one thing, but we physically practice quite another.

She further argues that women's bodies are especially docile, that women are spending more time than ever on the management and discipline of their bodies even as professional and political possibilities for women seem to be on the rise. She worries that the intensification of women's body regimens may be part of a kind of anti-feminist backlash, distracting and subverting women, and reasserting traditional gender configurations just as increased power is within their reach. She marvels at the durability and versatility of this normalization of the female body. All women, it seems, regardless of age, race, class, sexual orientation, or disability, are willing to invest considerable time and resources in taming their bodies.

Given this trend, Bordo argues that "we desperately need an effective political discourse about the female body."[10] For this discourse, she turns to Foucault and his insight that the central mechanisms of power are constitutive, not repressive. Power reproduces itself primarily by means of a network of practices, institutions and technologies, not by means of struggles between groups. (For a reminder of this, review Chapter 2.)

If women feel pressure to be beautiful, it is not because men force them to be beautiful but because the entire system in which we are embedded demands it at every corner. In order to understand the female body regimen, argues Bordo, we need to analyse the mechanisms through which our desires and practices are shaped, and through which our conceptions of normalcy and deviance emerge.

Bordo seeks to provide just such an analysis of three historically localized and typically female disorders—hysteria, agoraphobia, and anorexia nervosa. While Bordo admits that these three conditions primarily affect(ed) white, middle-age, middle class women, she hopes that her analysis will nonetheless provide a glimpse of the form that such analysis might take with other varieties of embodiment.

Bordo's analysis of all three conditions reveals two striking features: (1) in all three cases, the disorder in question reads as a caricature or parody of a dominant ideal for femininity during the relevant historical context, and (2) in all three disorders, we can see at once a resistance to dominant representations of the feminine and a capitulation to them.

12.3.1. The disorder as caricature

While one might be inclined to regard disorders as the opposite of normalcy, hysteria, agoraphobia, and anorexia nervosa all instead seem to occupy the same continuum with female normalcy. Normal women in the late nineteenth and early twentieth centuries were expected to be emotional and soft-spoken; in the hysteric, these traits are parodically exaggerated as wild mood swings and hysterical muteness. When, after World War II, the men returned to

---

10   Bordo, 15.

the factories, normal women were expected to resume their roles in the home; the agoraphobic took the ideal to the extreme in her refusal to leave the home. In our own time, the severe dieting of the anorexic is an extension of the ideal of the women who "eats like a bird." Thus, for Bordo, the symptoms of all three conditions are not merely symptoms but take on symbolic meanings that point to the system of power underlying the disorders. Thus, writes Bordo, "we find the body of the sufferer deeply inscribed with an ideological construction of femininity emblematic of the periods in question."[11] In this way, the bodies of disordered women serve as text-analogues susceptible of Foucauldian discursive analysis.

While Bordo uses the same mode of analysis on all three of the female conditions she considers, she sees hysteria's representation of feminine ideals as considerably more subtle than either agoraphobia's or anorexia's.

She explains the difference by means of the rise of visual culture. Since the mid-twentieth century, we have been constantly exposed to imagistic representations of femininity in film, magazines, television, and now the internet. Surrounded as we are by this physical imperative, she argues that we are more acutely than ever affected by gendered norms, and find it difficult to distinguish between parody and genuine possibilities for being.

12.3.2. The disorder as resistance and capitulation

Bordo continues that the disorders in question are not merely pathological exaggerations of cultural norms around femininity. They also constitute a form of silent resistance to those norms. To the stereotype of the woman dependent upon a man, Bordo sees the agoraphobic as retorting, "You want dependency? I'll give you dependency!"[12]

In this way, she argues, female disorders constitute a kind of "embodied protest—unconscious, inchoate, and counterproductive protest without an effective language, voice, or politics—but protest

---

11 Bordo, 16.
12 Bordo, 17.

nonetheless."[13] On this account, agoraphobia reads as resistance to the demand for women to run errands, drive their kids to school, accompany their husbands to events, and similar. Likewise, Bordo perceives the anorexic as pursuing feminine ideals "to the point where their destructive potential is revealed for all to see."[14]

As eloquent as such protest may be, however, Bordo also finds it counterproductive and self-defeating in that the symptoms of the disorders further disempower the sufferer, in the case of anorexia even threatening her life. On Bordo's account, this "protest and retreat in the same gesture" is inevitable whenever one employs "the language of femininity to protest the conditions of the female world"[15] since "the pathologies of female protest function, paradoxically, as if in collusion with the cultural conditions that produce them, reproducing rather than transforming precisely that which is being protested."[16]

12.4. Conclusion

Working through Hacking and Bordo helps us to understand both how wide the range of social construction theses is, and the critical, liberatory, and occasionally revolutionary force of such theses. It also brings us squarely back to some of the ideas we looked at in the first two chapters of this volume. Just as Foucault urged us to consider the mechanisms lurking behind our discursive practices and the practical uses to which those practices are put, Hacking and Bordo force us to examine both the sources and the applications of social construction claims.

If this volume has a moral it is that sex and gender claims and practices are never as simple as they might at first appear. While it is perhaps tempting to sort the human world into two tidy boxes—a pink one and a blue one—doing so risks effacing the real messiness of human sexuality. Entertaining a social constructivist hypothesis about sex and gender—whether we find that hypothesis ultimately convincing or not—allows us to question the inevitability

---

13   Bordo, 20.
14   Bordo, 21.
15   Bordo, 22.
16   Bordo, 22.

of binaristic categories in a way that clears a space for the real-life untidiness of sex and gender. Perhaps, if we're lucky, it makes us just a little more humble and kind in the process.

12.5. Questions for reflection

- Hacking urges us to focus on the possible pragmatic effects of social construction claims rather than on the content of the claims, to ask "why?" rather than "what?" Do you agree with this approach? Why or why not?
- Throughout, Bordo discusses the need to extend her analysis to other ethnic, racial, and class divisions. Can you think of historically local disorders that attend upon other groups besides middle-class white women? If so, do they admit of the same style of analysis as Bordo employs? Can you think of any such conditions that affect men?
- More broadly, how sympathetic are you to social construction theses as they apply to sex, gender, womanhood, manhood, femininity, and masculinity? On your view, how much of our gendered reality is socially constructed? How much is inevitable?
- Has reading this book changed your mind in any way about sex or gender? Which ideas or texts we considered will stay with you? Why?

12.6. Works cited and recommended reading

Bordo, Susan. "The Body and the Reproduction of Femininity: A Feminist Appropriation of Foucault." *Gender/Body/ Knowledge.* Ed. Alison Jaggar and Susan Bordo. New Brunswick, NJ: Rutgers University Press, 1989.

Bourdieu, Pierre. *Outline of a Theory of Practice.* Cambridge: Cambridge University Press, 1977.

Hacking, Ian. *The Social Construction of What?* Cambridge, MA: Harvard University Press, 1999.

Glossary

Accident: in Aristotle, a property that is not essential to a thing's nature.

Agender: a gender identity in which the person does not identify with any gender.

Aggressive: a member of an inner city, predominantly African American subculture of butch lesbians who adopt many aspects of traditionally masculine gender expression. Other terms used to express this gender expression include *AG* and *tomboi.*

Agoraphobia: an extreme fear of being in public.

Androcentrism: a perspective centred on men.

Androgyny: in Bem's Sex Role Inventory, expression of both highly masculine and highly feminine traits.

Aneuploidy: a mutation resulting in an unusual number of chromosomes. Thus, in sex chromosomes, more or fewer than two. XYY, for instance.

Anorexia nervosa: a serious illness in which sufferers regard themselves as fat and therefore engage in extreme diet and exercise.

Anthropocentrism: a perspective centred on human beings.

Anthropomorphism: the projection of human traits onto non-human animals and/or objects.

Asexual: the sexual orientation of people who do not feel sexual desire.

Bem Sex Role Inventory: a psychological measure of masculinity and femininity in which masculine and feminine are represented as two distinct axes rather than as the opposite ends of a single axis.

Binarism: the assumption of stable opposition, especially as relates to sex and gender.

Biodeterminism: the view that our fates are dictated by our biological make-up.

Camp: a playful, theatrical style of behaviour often associated with the gay male community.

Castration: the removal of the testes.

Cisgender: a way of describing people whose gender identity matches their gender assignment at birth.

Clitoromegaly: the condition of having an unusually large clitoris; clitoromegaly is associated with some intersex conditions.

Dimorphism: literally, *having two forms*. In sexually dimorphic species, the males and the females have different anatomies or appearances.

Dionian: in Karl Heinrich Ulrichs's system, the term for anyone who is not cis and straight.

Discursive practices: the things we say, verbally, in writing, and in text-analogues. Michel Foucault analyzes these in order to uncover systems of social power.

Documentary Hypothesis: the hypothesis that the Pentateuch was written in four distinct periods ranging from 900 BCE to 400 BCE. Also known as the Graf-Wellhausen Hypothesis.

Drag: playful cross-dressing, especially in performance.

Drag king/queen: one who engages in drag. Drag kings are typically women who dress as men, while drag queens are typically men who dress as women. However, drag does not always cross genders in this way. For instance, some trans men perform as drag kings.

Drapetomania: the now-rejected psychological diagnosis for African American slaves who wished to be free.

Écriture féminine: a mode of communication, especially writing, alleged by Luce Irigaray and Hélène Cixous to be characteristic of women's distinctive type of thought.

Endocrinology: the medical discipline concerned with hormones.

Enlightenment: a period in Western European thought, roughly 1650 to 1780. The period was characterized by revolutions in scientific, philosophical, religious, and political thought, and an optimism about the potential of human reason.

Epistemology: the branch of philosophy concerned with knowledge.

Essence: in Aristotle, a thing's core nature or definition.

Eugenics: a pseudo-science and social practice which imagined the genetic origin of all sorts of desirable and undesirable traits, and advocated the encouragement of people with the former to breed, and the discouragement (or prevention) of those with the latter from breeding. Eugenics is often associated with racism.

Evolutionary psychology: the branch of psychology that seeks to provide evolutionary explanations of psychological phenomena.

Existentialism: a philosophical school of thought holding that there is no objective meaning to life and that human beings can and must make life meaningful for themselves. Existentialists deny that human beings have an enduring essence. Instead, they argue that we become who we are through the choices we make.

Feminist essentialism: a variety of feminism that identifies certain traits and practices as distinctively feminine, and seeks to celebrate and support these traits and practices.

Form: in Aristotle, a thing's shape or type, as opposed to what that thing is composed of. See also *matter*.

Gender assignment: in Kessler and McKenna, the first gender attribution ever performed on a person, usually by a doctor or midwife. See also *gender attribution*.

Gender attribution: a decision about what gender someone is, usually made quickly and involuntarily. For Kessler and McKenna, gender attribution is the basis for all other gender concepts.

Gender dysphoria: the American Psychiatric Association's diagnostic term for trans people who experience distress because of their gender identity.

Gender identity: in Kessler and McKenna, a person's gender self-attribution. The gender one regards oneself as having.

Gender reassignment: in Kessler and McKenna, a "correction" to an incorrect gender assignment in the case of intersex infants. Kessler and McKenna prefer the term "gender reconstruction" because it more conveys that gender is constructed rather than discovered in such a case.

Gender role: in Kessler and McKenna, a prescription or proscription applied to people because of their gender. These may involve attire, modes of labour and recreation, political roles, etc. For example, in some cultures, women tend the children and wear pink.

Gender role-identity: in Kessler and McKenna, the attitude one has towards one's conventional gender role.

Genealogy: in Foucault, a method of discursive analysis that seeks to uncover how particular forms of discursive practice arise, and what leads us (apart from truth) to engage in these forms of discourse.

Genotype: an organism's genetic make-up. Contrasted with—see also—*phenotype*.

Germs: in Ulrichs's germ theory, all humans have imperceptible male or female internal aspects, present embryonically, that determine their sexual make-up and explain their sexual orientation.

GID: gender identity disorder—in the American Psychiatric Association's *Diagnostic and Statistical Manual* Ed. IV-TR, the diagnosis for adult trans people.

GID(C): gender identity disorder (child)—in the American Psychiatric Association's *Diagnostic and Statistical Manual* Ed. IV-TR, the diagnosis for juvenile trans people.

Gonad: the sex organ that produces gametes (eggs and sperm)—an ovary or a testicle.

Gonochoristic: the description for species in which more than one sex is required for reproduction, and in which people belong to only one sex for their entire lifespan.

Help-meet: a spouse whose role it is to help the other spouse. In Genesis 2:18, Eve is described as Adam's help-meet.

Hermaphrodite: 1. a member of a species that reproduces sexually, but in which individuals in the species may possess both sexes of sexual organs either at one time (simultaneous hermaphroditism) or over their lifespan (sequential hermaphroditism). 2. a term formerly used to refer to intersex people.

Heteronormative: assuming heterosexual norms and imposing them on others.

Hijra: a third-gender identity found on the Indian subcontinent.

Hysteria: a common nineteenth- and twentieth-century psychological diagnosis often made of women based on a wide range of symptoms. The diagnosis is now largely discounted.

Ideology: in neo-Marxism, a set of ideas, particular to a political system, that informs the thoughts, actions, and utterances of people living within that system without their being aware of it.

Implicit bias: a bias of which we are unaware, but which affects our conduct and judgment.

Indigeneity: the character of belonging to an indigenous population, aspects of that indigenous population.

Innate: present at birth, genetic rather than developmental.

Intersectionality: a mode of feminist analysis that considers multiple axes of oppression at the same time rather than focussing on a single axis.

Intersex: born with both male and female biological characteristics, or with ambiguous sex organs.

Kinsey scale: Alfred Kinsey's Heterosexual-Homosexual Rating Scale, an instrument designed to measure subjects' sexual orientation. The Kinsey scale assumes that homosexuals, bisexuals, and heterosexuals differ by degree rather than by kind.

Lesbian separatism: a variety of feminist separatism that advocates for women to live and work separately from men and to pursue lesbian relationships.

LGBTTIQQ2S: one of several similar acronyms for the lesbian, gay, bisexual, transsexual, transgender, intersex, queer, questioning, and two-spirited community.

Matter: in Aristotle, what a thing is composed of, as opposed to its shape or type. See also *form*.

Metaphysics: the branch of philosophy concerned with the character of reality and existence.

Morphological: relating to a thing's form or structure. Also, *morphology*.

MTF/FTM: Male-to-female/female-to-male, a means of identifying trans people that is increasingly falling into disuse.

Natural kind: a group or type that is both natural (that is, not a human product or perception) and a genuine kind (as opposed to an arbitrary grouping). Many philosophers consider chemical elements and compounds to be natural kinds. There is greater disagreement over whether biological groups such as species or sexes constitute natural kinds.

Natural selection: the process posited by Darwin as the main mechanism of evolution. In natural selection, organisms well adapted to their environments live longer than less well adapted organisms, and hence are able to reproduce more often than them. This results in more offspring carrying the adaptation in their genes.

Naturalistic fallacy: an error in reasoning in which a phenomenon's goodness is inferred from its naturalness (or other supposed descriptive facts).

Nominalism: the metaphysical position that laws, types, and general ideas are not real, and that names of types of things merely group them arbitrarily. See also *realism*.

Normative: having to do with value judgments or prescriptions. Often opposed to "descriptive." Descriptive utterances merely express what is the case; normative judgments seek to communicate what *ought to be* the case.

Oedipal stage: in Freud, a developmental stage at which young boys reject their fathers and desire their mothers; after the Greek mythological figure, Oedipus, who killed his father and married his mother.

Paraphilia: in psychiatry, a condition characterized by unhealthy sexual desires.

Parthenogenesis: reproduction by means of an unfertilized ovum; reproduction with the genetic material of only one parent.

Pathologize: to treat something as unhealthy.

Pediatrics: the medical specialization concerned with treating babies and children.

Penectomy: the surgical removal of the penis.

Phallocratism: government by males (literally, those with phalluses).

Phallus: a penis, or penis shaped object.

Phenotype: an organism's observable physical characteristics (anatomy, for instance) and behaviour; contrasted with—see also—*genotype*.

Phenotypical: relating to the phenotype.

Proletariat: in Marxism, the urban working class.

Realism: the metaphysical position that laws, types, and general ideas are real. Contrasted with—see also—*nominalism*.

Relativism: the position that knowledge, reality, or goodness is relative to the observer, not absolute.

Science wars: an intellectual controversy that was waged in the 1990s between social constructivists about science and those—both nominalists and realists—who opposed the application of the social construction hypothesis to science.

Seeing-as: the kind of seeing that already involves judgment or interpretation, as opposed to the mere naked perception of visual data.

Sexual selection: the mechanism described by Darwin as the source of sexual dimorphism. In sexual selection, those traits that make males more attractive to females make those males more reproductively successful. Hence, those traits (e.g., red feathers) are passed on to the next generation.

Shamanism: traditional beliefs and practices centred on the shaman, a priestly figure who is believed to be able to travel between the material world and the world of spirits.

Social constructivism: the view that the phenomenon in question is the product of social conditions and values, and therefore not inevitable.

Somatic: relating to the body.

SRS: sex reassignment surgery. A broad class of surgical procedures performed on trans people to enable them to live in the bodies they identify with. Sometimes termed *gender confirmation surgery.*

Taxonomy: a systemic classification, typically of organisms.

Trans: transgender, having a gender identity that does not align with one's gender assignment at birth.

Trans*: a variation on "trans" intended to convey greater inclusiveness.

Transfeminism: a variety of feminism, often practiced by trans women, that seeks to include the experiences and concerns of trans people.

Transsexual: a now mostly disused term for a transgender person who has undergone or is undergoing sex reassignment.

Transvestism: the practice of dressing as the "opposite sex," either for recreational or ritual reasons.

Transvestite: someone who dresses as the "opposite sex," either for their own pleasure or for ritual reasons.

Two spirit: a North American indigenous gender identity in which people feel like they have both male and female spirits.

Uranian: in Ulrichs, the term for anyone who is not straight and cisgender.

Urology: the branch of medicine concerned with the genitourinary tract.

Vaginal agenesis: a physical condition in which a fetus's vagina does not fully develop.

Annotated Bibliography

American Psychiatric Association. *Diagnostic and Statistical Manual of Mental Disorders: DSM-5*. Arlington, VA: American Psychiatric Publishing, 2013.
   The latest edition of the American Psychiatric Association's diagnostic manual. Each edition of this manual incorporates a number of key changes to diagnoses. The DSM-5 drops the previous edition's diagnostic categories of Gender Identity Disorder and Gender Identity Disorder–Child in favour of Gender Dysphoria.

American Psychiatric Association. "Gender Dysphoria." 2013. <http://www.dsm5.org/documents/gender%20dysphoria%20 fact%20sheet.pdf>
   A brief fact-sheet summarizing the new DSM-5 approach to Gender Dysphoria (formally Gender Identity Disorder).

Aquinas, Saint Thomas. *The Disputed Questions on Truth*. Vol. 1. Qu. 5, art. 9, d. 9. *The Collected Works of St. Thomas Aquinas*, electronic edition. Charlottesville: Intelex, 1993.
   In this text, highly influential Roman Catholic Church theologian/ philosopher St. Thomas Aquinas discusses how women

are created and why they are different from men. His view recapitulates the earlier Aristotelian position on the matter.

Aristotle. Book X, Chapter 9. *Metaphysics*. *The Basic Works of Aristotle*. Ed. Richard McKeon. New York: Random House, 1941.
Ancient Greek philosopher Aristotle here puzzles over how it is that men and women can be so different and yet belong to the same species.

Aristotle. *Generation of Animals*. Trans. A.L. Peck. London: Heinemann, 1943.
Aristotle's account of sexual reproduction, and his explanation of sexual dimorphism, this fascinating ancient foray into reproductive biology was a major influence on medieval Christian accounts of sex and gender.

Augustine, Saint. *On the Trinity*. Book XII, Chapter VII. *Basic Writings of Saint Augustine*. Vol. 2. Ed. W.J. Oates. New York: Random House, 1948.
In this text, early Church father St. Augustine works to reconcile Genesis 1's egalitarian account of the creation of man and woman with the Apostle Paul's injunction to women to cover their heads and to men to bare theirs. Augustine's solution to the apparent tension between these two texts bears traces of Aristotle's thoughts on sex and gender.

Baron-Cohen, Simon. *The Essential Difference: Men, Women and the Extreme Male Brain*. New York: Basic, 2004.
Neuroscientist Baron-Cohen's popular elaboration of his "extreme male brain theory," which holds that, in general, men are systemizers, women are empathizers, and autism resembles extreme instances of male systemizing thought.

Beauvoir, Simone de. *The Second Sex*. Trans. Constance Borde and Sheila Malovany-Chevallier. New York: Vintage, 2011.
The authoritative translation of Beauvoir's classic feminist existentialist study. Beauvoir argues that women are socially constructed, not naturally occurring, and that at the heart of this social construction is a marginalization of woman as the Other to man's One.

Bem, Sandra. "The Measurement of Psychological Androgyny." *Journal of Clinical and Consulting Psychology* 42 (1974): 155–62.

Psychologist Sandra Bem's first elaboration of her influential theory that masculinity and femininity are not opposites, but are rather orthogonal to each other. For Bem, a person can be highly masculine and highly feminine, low in both femininity and masculinity, or high in one and low in the other. For Bem, the combination of high masculinity with high femininity is androgyny.

Benjamin, Harry. *The Transsexual Phenomenon*. New York: Julian Press, 1966.

A sympathetic discussion of transgenderism by an endocrinologist who was an important early champion of sex reassignment surgery.

Blackless, Melanie et al. "How Sexually Dimorphic Are We? Review and Synthesis." *American Journal of Human Biology* 12 (2000): 151–66.

A survey of varieties of intersex, with statistical data about the incidence of each variety, from biologist Anne Fausto-Sterling's research team.

Bluhm, Robyn, Ann Jaap Jacobson, and Heidi Lene Maibom, Eds. *Neurofeminism: Issues at the Intersection of Feminist Theory and Cognitive Science*. London: Palgrave-Macmillan, 2012.

A collection of essays by some of the pioneers of neurofeminism.

Bordo, Susan. "The Body and the Reproduction of Femininity: A Feminist Appropriation of Foucault." *Gender/Body/Knowledge*. Ed. Alison Jaggar and Susan Bordo. New Brunswick, NJ: Rutgers University Press, 1989.

Philosopher Susan Bordo extends Foucauldian discursive analysis to the body, arguing that close attention to gendered pathologies reveals them as the tragic effects of gender as a system of power.

Borges, Jorge Luis. "The Analytical Language of John Wilkins." *Other Inquisitions: 1937–1952*. Trans. Ruth Simms. London: Souvenir Press, 1973. 101–05.

A whimsical fictitious essay that illustrates some of the puzzles associated with classification. Inspiration for Foucault in *The Order of Things*.

Bourdieu, Pierre. *Outline of a Theory of Practice*. Cambridge: Cambridge University Press, 1977.
In this rich and complex volume, French sociologist Pierre Bourdieu elaborates his account of *habitus*, Bourdieu's term for the mechanism whereby we embody and thereby reinforce the prevailing system of power, without even being conscious of it. Bourdieu's view that culture can inscribe itself on the body is an important influence on Bordo.

Burkett, Elinor. "What Makes a Woman?" *New York Times*, online edition. 6 June 2015. <http://www.nytimes.com/2015/06/07/opinion/sunday/what-makes-a-woman.html?_r=0>
In this provocative, controversial response to Caitlyn Jenner's highly publicized announcement that she is a woman, filmmaker Elinor Burkett arguably exemplifies some aspects of radical feminism. The column was received angrily by trans people and their allies, who regarded it as an instance of transphobia.

Buss, David. "Psychological Sex Differences: Origins Through Sexual Selection." *American Psychologist* 50.3 (1995): 164–68.
A classic evolutionary psychology account of the evolutionary basis of various sex differences between men and women.

Butler, Judith. *Gender Trouble: Feminism and the Subversion of Identity*. New York: Routledge, 1990.
Philosopher and cultural theorist Judith Butler's ground-breaking study of the social construction of sex and gender. Butler regards gender as a performance—something we do rather than a stable category that defines us, and advocates for the subversive, liberatory potential of consciously playing with our gender performances.

Califia, Patrick. *Sex Changes: Transgender Politics*. 2nd ed. Berkeley: Cleis Press, 2003.
A smart, trenchant study of trans politics with special attention to the history of trans identities, and the often-fraught relationship between trans people and cis-feminists and lesbians.

Canadian Institutes of Health Research—Institute of Gender and Health. *What a Difference Sex and Gender Make: A Gender,*

Sex and Health Research Casebook. <http://www.cihr-irsc.
gc.ca/e/44734.html>
An online anthology of useful discussions of the role of sex and
gender in health research from Canada's federal health research
institute.

Cobb, Matthew. *Generation: The Seventeenth-Century Scientists
Who Unraveled the Secrets of Sex, Life, and Growth.* New
York: Bloomsbury, 2006.
An accessible, scientifically well-informed history of the fascinating path seventeenth-century scientists took on the way to the
discovery of how the sperm and egg combine in reproduction.
This book provides a snapshot into just how much reproductive
biology has advanced in the past four hundred years, and how
very different pre-seventeenth accounts of reproductive biology
were from our contemporary one.

Crenshaw, Kimberlé. "Demarginalizing the Intersection of Race
and Sex: A Black Feminist Critique of Antidiscrimination
Doctrine, Feminist Theory and Antiracist Politics." *The
University of Chicago Legal Forum* 140 (1989): 139–67.
This is the classic, original expression of intersectionality, a
framework that allows theorists to understand injustice as
simultaneously operating on multiple axes with respect to the
same person.

D'Anglure, Bernard Saladin. "The 'Third Gender' of the Inuit."
Diogenes 208 (2005): 134–44.
A Canadian anthropologist's study of religious and economic
transvestism among the Inuit.

Darwin, Charles. *Descent of Man, and Selection in Relation to
Sex.* Princeton, NJ: Princeton University Press, 1981.
Darwin's full expression of his theory of sexual selection, which
explains the evolutionary basis for sexual dimorphism.

Daston, Lorraine and Peter Galison. "The Image of Objectivity."
Representations 40 (Fall 1992): 81–128.
A classic analysis of the rise of competing conceptualizations of
objectivity in the history of science, and the way in which those
sometimes mutually-inconsistent conceptualizations are entangled
in our contemporary understanding of objectivity.

Deslauriers, Marguerite. "Sex Difference and Essence in
     Aristotle's Metaphysics and Biology." *Feminist Interpretations
     of Aristotle*. Ed. Cynthia Freeland. University Park:
     Pennsylvania State University Press, 1998. 138–67.
     A study of the inconsistencies among Aristotle's accounts of sex
     difference in several of his works.
Dreger, Alice. *Hermaphrodites and the Medical Invention of Sex*.
     Cambridge, MA: Harvard University Press, 1998.
     Sex scholar Alice Dreger's study of the history of intersex, and
     of the shifts between successive historical understandings of and
     reactions to intersex.
Dworkin, Andrea. *Intercourse*. New York: Free Press, 1987.
     Feminist scholar Andrea Dworkin's classic argument that
     heterosexual sex is intrinsically violent and hierarchical in
     character.
Fausto-Sterling, Anne. "The Five Sexes: Why Male and Female
     are Not Enough." *Sciences* (March/April 1993): 20–24.
     Sex scientist Anne Fausto-Sterling's classic argument to the effect
     that the varieties of intersex necessitate not two sexes, but five.
Feder, Ellen and Katrina Karkazis. "What's in a Name: The
     Controversy over 'Disorders of Sex Development.'" *Hastings
     Center Report* 38.5 (2008): 33–36.
     A thoughtful defence of the 2006 decision by a group of
     physicians and intersex activists to adopt the term "disorders of
     sex development" instead of "intersex" for clinical uses.
Fine, Cordelia. *Delusions of Gender: How Our Minds, Society,
     and Neurosexism Create Difference*. New York: Norton, 2010.
     Feminist neuroscientist Cordelia Fine's debunking of
     neuroscientific and psychological arguments that there are male
     brains and female brains.
Firestone, Shulamith. *The Dialectic of Sex: The Case For
     Feminist Revolution*. New York: Morrow, 1970.
     In this classic and highly influential radical feminist work,
     the author attributes all social inequalities to the biological
     burdens reproduction imposes on women. She proposes modern
     technology as the solution to this widespread inequality.
Foucault, Michel. *The History of Sexuality*. Vol. 1. Trans. Robert
     Hurley. New York: Random House, 1978.

French sociologist and philosopher Michel Foucault's ground-breaking study of the history of sexual desire, sexual orientation, and sexual mores and conduct.

Foucault, Michel. *The Order of Things: An Archaeology of the Human Sciences*. New York: Vintage, 1994.
Foucault's highly influential genealogy of the social sciences. This volume is an excellent place to start when thinking about the conventions and applications of classification, especially the classification of human beings and their behaviour.

Freud, Sigmund. "Some Psychical Consequences of the Anatomical Distinction between the Sexes." *The Standard Edition of the Complete Psychological Works of Sigmund Freud*. Vol. 19. Trans. James Strachey. London: Hogarth Press, 1961. 248–58.
A late work by the father of psychoanalysis, in which he seeks to explain the anatomical basis for some alleged psychological and behavioural differences between males and females.

Gilligan, Carol. *In a Different Voice: Psychological Theory and Women's Development*. Cambridge, MA: Harvard University Press, 1993.
In this classic volume, psychologist Carol Gilligan argues that women's moral judgment is grounded on relations, unlike men's, which is grounded in abstract principles.

Grant, Jaime, Lisa Mottet, Justin Tanis, et al. *Injustice at Every Turn: A Report of the National Transgender Discrimination Survey*. Washington, DC: The National Gay and Lesbian Task Force and the National Center for Transgender Equality, 2011. <http://www.transequality.org/sites/default/files/docs/resources/NTDS_Report.pdf.>
A thorough survey and analysis of discrimination faced by American trans people and the effect of this discrimination on their well-being.

Groneberg, Michael. "Myth and Science around Gender and Sexuality: Eros and the Three Sexes in Plato's Symposium." *Diogenes* 208 (2005): 39–49.
An account of the Aristophanic myth from Plato's *Symposium*, and its influence on Ulrichs, Hirschfeld, and Freud.

Gulati, Martha and Henry R. Black. "Heart Rate Response to
Exercise Stress Testing in Asymptomatic Women: The St. James
Women Take Heart Project." *Circulation* 122.2 (2010): 130–37.
A study that made international news with its revelation that wom-
en's maximum heart rate is lower than men's, and that physicians,
personal trainers, etc. had been putting women's safety at risk by
assuming that their maximum heart rate is the same as men's.

Hacking, Ian. *The Social Construction of What?* Cambridge,
MA: Harvard University Press, 1999.
Prompted by the so-called science wars, Hacking offers a careful
analysis of the several varieties of social constructivism.

Haslanger, Sally. "Gender and Race: (What) Are They? (What)
Do We Want Them to Be?" *Noûs* 34.1 (2000): 31–55.
A classic work in which the feminist philosopher elaborates her
view that the very definitions of "man" and "woman" already
have power relations built into them.

Holmes, Morgan. *Intersex: A Perilous Difference.* Selinsgrove,
PA: Susquehanna University Press, 2008.
An analysis by Canadian intersex scholar and activist Morgan
Holmes of the treatment of intersex people and of the cultural
basis of that treatment.

hooks, bell. "Understanding Patriarchy." *The Will to Change:
Men, Masculinity, and Love.* New York: Atria, 2004. 17–34.
An influential essay in which Black feminist bell hooks argues that
men too are disadvantaged by patriarchy.

Hubbard, Ruth. "Have Only Men Evolved?" Reprinted in
Hubbard, *The Politics of Women's Biology.* New Brunswick,
NJ: Rutgers, 1990. 87–106.
A feminist biologist's criticism of the androcentrism of traditional
evolutionary theory.

Intersex Society of North America website. <www.isna.org>
The archived website of the now-defunct activist group. An
excellent repository of resources on intersex issues.

Irigaray, Luce. "This Sex Which Is Not One." *This Sex Which Is
Not One.* Ithaca, NY: Cornell University Press, 1985. 23–33.
A classic expression of écriture féminine, the feminist essentialist
mode of communication pioneered by Luce Irigaray and Hélène
Cixous.

Jorgensen, Christine. *Christine Jorgensen: A Personal Autobiography*. New York: Bantam, 1967.
The poignant autobiography of a trans pioneer.
Kessler, Suzanne. "The Medical Construction of Gender: Case Management of Intersexed Infants." *Signs* 16.1 (1990): 3–26.
A report on interviews with various specialists treating intersex patients in the 1980s.
Kessler, Suzanne and Wendy McKenna. *Gender: An Ethnomethodological Approach*. Chicago: University of Chicago Press, 1978.
A classic study in which the authors argue that gender is actually the umbrella term for a number of more precise terms, each of them variations on the act of gender attribution.
Kinsey Institute. *Kinsey's Heterosexual-Homosexual Rating Scale*. <http://www.kinseyinstitute.org/research/ak-hhscale.html>
The famous instrument for measuring the degree of a subject's hetero-bi-homosexuality.
Laqueur, Thomas. *Making Sex: Body and Gender from the Greeks to Freud*. Cambridge, MA: Harvard University Press, 1990.
A study in the history of medicine arguing for the social construction of biological sex.
Lee, Peter et al. "Consensus Statement on Management of Intersex Disorders." *Pediatrics* 118.2 (2006): e488–e500.
This consensus statement was jointly produced by medical practitioners, intersex people, and activists. It stipulates new, mutually agreed-upon clinical guidelines for the treatment of intersex conditions.
Martino, Mario. *Emergence: A Transsexual Autobiography*. New York: Crown Publishers, 1977.
An autobiography of a trans pioneer.
McCarthy, Cormac. *Outer Dark*. New York: Vintage, 1993.
A Southern Gothic novel with philosophical overtones.
Money, John and Anke Ehrhardt. *Man & Woman, Boy & Girl*. Baltimore, MD: Johns Hopkins University Press, 1972.
This highly influential work articulated protocols for the treatment of intersex patients; these protocols, now largely rejected, remained more or less in effect until the early 2000s.

Morgan, Elaine. *The Descent of Woman*. London: Souvenir Press, 1972.
  A classic work that both criticizes androcentric evolutionary theory, and offers a woman-centred alternative—the Aquatic Ape Hypothesis.

Morris, Jan. *Conundrum*. New York: Harcourt, Brace, Jovanovich, 1974.
  An insightful and engagingly written memoir by a trans pioneer.

Nanda, Serena. "The Hijras of India." *A Queer World*. Ed. Martin Duberman. New York: New York University Press, 1997. 82–86.
  An early study on hijras, their origin, and practices.

Overall, Christine. "Return to Gender, Address Unknown: Reflections on the Past, Present, and Future of the Concept of Gender in Feminist Theory and Practice." *Marginal Groups and Mainstream American Culture*. Ed. Yolanda Estes, Arnold Farr, Patricia Smith, and Clelia Smyth. Lawrence: University Press of Kansas, 2000. 24–50.
  A feminist philosophy argument tracing the history of the concept of gender, and arguing that we ought to abandon the notion of gender in order to liberate people from the constraints of gender.

Peddle, Daniel, dir. *The Aggressives*. Seventh Art Releasing, 2005.
  A documentary film about a predominantly African American subculture of lesbians who identify as women but who adopt male gender roles, deriving their identity as *aggressives* from their performance of a stereotypical version of Black masculinity.

Pinker, Steven. *The Blank Slate: The Modern Denial of Human Nature*. New York: Penguin, 2002.
  A highly popular argument against social constructivism, the volume draws on cognitive science, neuroscience, and evolutionary psychology. The chapter on gender offers a thorough catalogue of various, mostly scientific arguments against the social construction of gender and gender roles.

Plato. *Symposium. Great Dialogues of Plato*. Ed. Eric Warmington and Phillip Rouse. Trans. W.H.D. Rouse. New York: Mentor, 1956. 69–117.
  This Platonic dialogue introduces the myth of the three sexes, as well as the source of the romantic notion of a soulmate.

Richardson, Sarah. *Sex Itself: The Search for Male and Female in the Human Genome*. Chicago: University of Chicago Press, 2013.
A feminist philosopher of science considers the range of extant scientific evidence suggesting that males and females might be different at the level of genetics.

Roscoe, Will. *Changing Ones: Third and Fourth Genders in Native North America*. New York: St. Martin's Press, 1998.
An important study of non-binary gender identities in North American indigenous cultures.

Roughgarden, Joan. *Evolution's Rainbow: Diversity, Gender, and Sexuality in Nature and People*. Berkeley: University of California Press, 2004.
A distinguished evolutionary biologist's often polemical survey of sexual diversity in the natural world.

Rousseau, Jean-Jacques. *Emilius and Sophia: Or, A New System of Education*. 2nd ed. Vol. 4. London: Becket and Hondt, 1763.
A classic treatise on the education of children that, in the final volume, contrasts the natures of girls and boys, and argues for a different approach to educating each of the sexes.

Rousseau, Jean-Jacques. *An Inquiry into the Nature of the Social Contract; or Principles of Political Right*. Dublin: Jones, 1791.
Rousseau here elaborates his famous social contract theory, as well as his diagnosis of human bondage.

Sax, L. "How Common Is Intersex? A Response to Anne Fausto-Sterling." *Journal of Sex Research* 39.3 (August 2002): 174–78.
This article seeks to debunk the data on the incidence of intersex produced by Anne Fausto-Sterling's lab.

Serano, Julia. "Trans-misogyny primer." N.d. Julia Serano website. <http://www.juliaserano.com/av/TransmisogynyPrimer-Serano.pdf>
An accessible and useful primer on transmisogyny by the author of that concept.

Serano, Julia. *Whipping Girl: A Transsexual Woman on Sexism and the Scapegoating of Femininity*. Emeryville, CA: Seal Press, 2007.
Serano's influential transfeminist manifesto.

Shelley, Mary. *Frankenstein; or, The Modern Prometheus*. Ed. Susan J. Wolfson. New York: Pearson Longman, 2007.

This famous novel written by Mary Wollstonecraft's daughter, Mary Shelley, shows traces of Rousseau's influence on the family.

Weissmann, Jordan. "Female Crash Dummies Part of Updated Vehicle Safety Tests." *The Washington Post* 9 July 2008. <http://www.washingtonpost.com/wp-dyn/content/article/2008/07/08/AR2008070802661.html?hpid=sec-business&sslid=33252>
A news story reporting the (then) new law under which automobile manufacturers would be obliged to conduct safety tests with female as well as male dummies.

Witt, Charlotte. *The Metaphysics of Gender*. Oxford: Oxford University Press, 2011.
A recent philosophical monograph that draws upon historical arguments from Aristotle to John Locke to elaborate an account of gender as a properly social category (rather than a category that is proper to species or to persons).

Wittgenstein, Ludwig. *Philosophical Investigations*. 4th ed. Ed. and trans. P.M.S. Hacker and Joachim Schulte. Oxford: Wiley-Blackwell, 2009.
The classic locus of Wittgenstein's *seeing-as* concept.

Wollstonecraft, Mary. *A Vindication of the Rights of Men and a Vindication of the Rights of Woman*. Cambridge: Cambridge University Press, 1995.
Two classic Enlightenment texts by an important early feminist. The first text argues for the equal treatment, and in particular the equal liberty, of all men. The second text extends the argument to include women.

Index

From the Publisher

A name never says it all, but the word "Broadview" expresses a good deal of the philosophy behind our company. We are open to a broad range of academic approaches and political viewpoints. We pay attention to the broad impact book publishing and book printing has in the wider world; we began using recycled stock more than a decade ago, and for some years now we have used 100% recycled paper for most titles. Our publishing program is internationally oriented and broad-ranging. Our individual titles often appeal to a broad readership too; many are of interest as much to general readers as to academics and students.

Founded in 1985, Broadview remains a fully independent company owned by its shareholders—not an imprint or subsidiary of a larger multinational.

For the most accurate information on our books (including information on pricing, editions, and formats) please visit our website at www.broadviewpress.com. Our print books and ebooks are also available for sale on our site.

On the Broadview website we also offer several goods that are not books—among them the Broadview coffee mug, the Broadview beer stein (inscribed with a line from Geoffrey Chaucer's *Canterbury Tales*), the Broadview fridge magnets (your choice of philosophical or literary), and a range of T-shirts (made from combinations of hemp, bamboo, and/or high-quality pima cotton, with no child labor, sweatshop labor, or environmental degradation involved in their manufacture).

All these goods are available through the "merchandise" section of the Broadview website. When you buy Broadview goods you can support other goods too.

broadview press
www.broadviewpress.com

The interior of this book is printed on 100% recycled paper.